UTOPIAN CRAFTSMEN

UTOPIAN CRAFTSMEN

The Arts and Crafts Movement from the Cotswolds to Chicago

LIONEL LAMBOURNE

Peregrine Smith, Inc.

SALT LAKE CITY

1980

To
Major and Mrs Anthony Biddulph
and
Mr and Mrs Donald Gimson,
who have made me, and many others, welcome in
their houses, which are among the finest
achievements of the Arts and Crafts movement

Frontispiece One of the members of Eric Gill's Catholic Guild of
Craftsmen devoted to St. Joseph and St. Dominic at 'Piggott's',
Buckinghamshire in 1940. Like Pugin and Morris before him, Gill
(1882–1940) admired the mediaeval craft system. In his old age he
wrote, 'Above all things (I hope) that I have done something towards
reintegrating bed and board, the small farm and the workshop, the
home and the school, earth and heaven.' These words can stand as an
epigraph for the lives and aspirations of the men and women whose
stories are told in this book.
Illustration: BBC Hulton Picture Library

First published in 1980 by Astragal Books, an imprint of The
Architectural Press Ltd: London

Published in the United States of America by Peregrine Smith, Inc:
Salt Lake City

Library of Congress Cataloguing in Publication Data
Lambourne, Lionel.
  Utopian Craftsmen.
  Bibliography:
  Include Index.
  1. Arts and Crafts Movement—History.
  I. Title.
  NK 1140.L35 745 80-17889
  ISBN 0-87905-080-2

Filmset and printed in Great Britain by
BAS Printers Limited,
Over Wallop, Hampshire

Contents

Acknowledgements

I would like to thank the following people for their help during the preparation of this book: David Coachworth, Mary Comino of Cheltenham Art Gallery, Margaret Crowther, editor, Richard Dennis, Julia Elliott, who first suggested the idea of the book, Norah Gillow of the William Morris Gallery, Mrs. F. L. M. Griggs, Gillian Naylor, Barley Roscoe of the Craft Study Centre, Bath, Peyton Skipwith of the Fine Art Society and my colleagues at the V and A, Michael Snodin for his valuable advice and Moira Walters for taking most of the photographs.

I am most grateful to Godfrey Golzen, who commissioned the book, for his patient advice, without which it would never have been completed.

Notes on Borders and Decorative Tail-pieces

Title page   Tail-piece designed by Herbert P. Horne, from the *Hobby Horse*. (This tailpiece is repeated throughout the book)

Page 1   Border for the Kelmscott Press edition of John Ruskin's 'The Nature of Gothic', designed by William Morris

Page 16   Tail-piece designed by Herbert P. Horne, from the *Hobby Horse*

Page 17   Border from the Kelmscott Press Chaucer, 'The Prologue of the Tail of the Manne of Lawe', designed by William Morris

Page 34   Tail-piece designed by Herbert P. Horne for the *Hobby Horse*

Page 35   Border by Bernard Pictor from Erhardt Ratdolt's *Appianus*, 1477, selected by Herbert P. Horne for the Riccardi Press edition of Shakespeare's *Sonnets*. Surprisingly, though the *Hobby Horse* magazine was embellished with numerous tail-pieces and decorative initials designed by Horne, A. H. Mackmurdo and Selwyn Image, borders were not used. The tail-piece is the colophon of the Century Guild

Page 52   Tail-piece by Herbert P. Horne from the *Hobby Horse*

Page 53   Border from a prospectus of the Kelmscott Press, designed by William Morris

Page 72   Tail-piece by Herbert P. Horne from the *Hobby Horse*

Page 73   Border designed by William Morris for *The Dream of John Ball*

Page 101   Border designed by Peter Behrens for Richard Booth's *Reiseführer*

Page 123   C. R. Ashbee's Essex House Press publications had no decorative borders. This device was inspired by the pinks which grew in the garden of Essex House in the Mile End Road

Page 145   Decorative border from the catalogue of the first Boston Arts and Crafts Exhibition

Page 163   The Eragny Press border designed by Lucien Pissarro for S. T. Coleridge's *Christabel*. Pissarro shared with Gimson an observant eye for the stylized pattern opportunities provided by leaves and tendrils

Page 189   Tail-piece from an early Heal and Sons catalogue

Page 193   Border by May Smith from *The Pretty Picture Book*, 1933

Page 201   Art deco border, origin unknown, *c.* 1930

Page 212   The tail-piece is a design for a fire-dog finial by Ernest Gimson (Cheltenham Art Gallery)

All the initial capital letters are woodcuts from the *Hobby Horse* with the exception of page 124, where the initial C is from C. R. Ashbee's alphabet of pinks

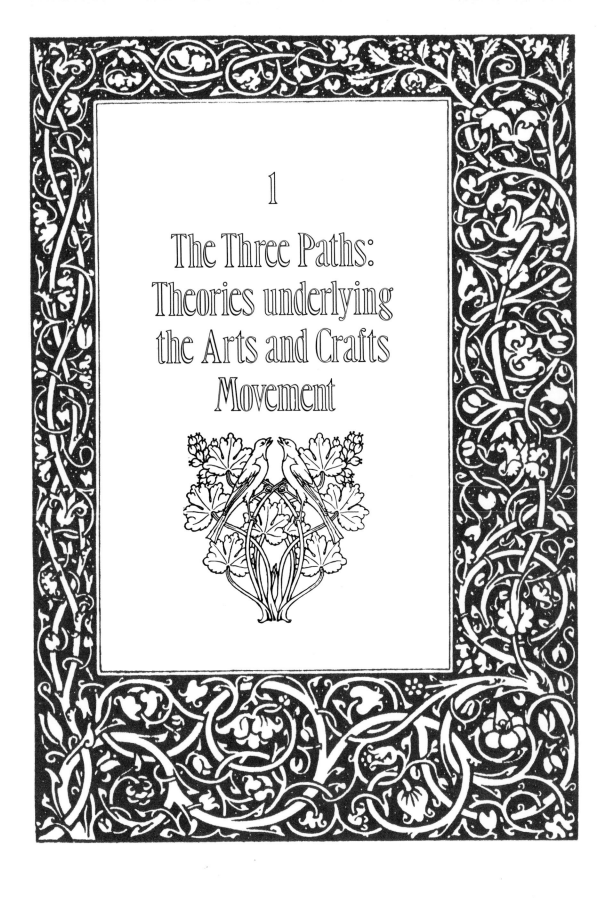

1

The Three Paths: Theories underlying the Arts and Crafts Movement

IR OSBERT LANCASTER's delightful book, *Home, Sweet Homes*, published in 1939, provides a witty and succinct description of the meaning still conjured up for many non-specialist readers by the words 'Arts and Crafts Movement'. He wrote 'Ever since the 'eighties in the byways of Chelsea and the lost vallies of the Cotswolds a handful of devoted Artists and Craftsmen had been living the simple life according to the doctrines of William Morris, surrounded by hand-woven linens, vegetable dyed, and plain unstained oak furniture by "goode workmen wel ywrought".'

Since these satirical words were written much has changed. The Art Nouveau and Art Deco revivals have come, and, surprisingly, stayed, and interest has now been reawakened in the Arts and Crafts movement. This reappraisal is in part related to our current concern with the ecological and environmental problems of the twentieth century which make us view the nineteenth-century preoccupations with the effects of industrialism with a new sympathy. The Arts and Crafts movement's attempt to combat these problems have on re-examination a new validity.

This said, Sir Osbert Lancaster's summary, like all good satires, contains an uncomfortable amount of truth. The 'simple life' adopted by many figures in the movement had its ridiculous side, and so did some of the works which they produced. These qualities were inevitably seized on by *Punch* with its sharp eye for fashionable trends in a cartoon by Lewis Baumer of 1903 (see Figs. 1 and 2). The 'artful' and 'crafty' connotations in the movement's cumbersome title have passed into popular speech in the pejorative phrase 'arty-crafty'.

1 *The Discomfiture of the Philistines. On Being Presented with Artful and Crafty Puzzle by Artistic Friend. (Query—Is it the Right Way Up?).* Caricature by Lewis Baumer, *Punch*, 1903

THE DISCOMFITURE OF THE PHILISTINES.
(On being presented with artful and crafty Puzzle by Artistic Friend. (Query—Is it the right way up? And, if so, what is it?)

2

2 Cabinet, Liberty and Company, probably designed by L. Wyburd (Bowes Museum, Barnard Castle)

Yet the achievements of the movement were far from negligible, and its effects on subsequent twentieth-century life profound. But before its course can be charted it is first necessary to examine the growing dominance of the machine and the parallel development of a deep rooted intellectual distrust of its effect on society in 19th-century England.

The beginnings of the industrial revolution in the eighteenth century were at first confined to accelerating the processes of manufacture in the cotton industry. Hargreave's 'Spinning Jenny' in 1764, which enabled one hand to attend to a number of spindles; Richard Arkwright's 'Water-frame' which produced a much stronger yarn, and Samuel Crompton's 'Mule' which spun the yarn much finer enabling muslin to be produced, were all at first powered by water-driven machinery. But with the growing elaboration of machinery came the need for a more concentrated form of energy, and the development of the steam engine.

Thus machines grew larger and more complicated, and the old cottage industries were starved out, after bitter struggles for survival. As G. K. Chesterton pointed out, the word 'master' ceased to mean a man who was master of his craft and came to mean a man who was master of others. The more enterprising of the hand workers set up as manufacturers on a large scale, the less enterprising, or less fortunate, the overwhelming majority of the population, became mere machine minders.

With the coming of the age of steam a corresponding change took place in farming methods. The movement of population to the towns to spend their days in machine minding led to a demand for increasing production from the soil, and the emergence of larger farming units and more highly mechanized and productive agricultural methods.

In both town and country some, more militant, spirits rebelled against the tyranny of machine labour, and played out the abortive role of destroying the machines, notably the Luddites in 1811, and the rural machine wreckers of the 1830s. A writer like William Cobbett (1762–1835) born into the old yeoman-farmer class, but turned radical because of his dislike of the effects of the industrial revolution, looked back nostalgically to the happy days when 'bread and meat, not wretched potatoes, were the food of the labouring people'. His writings, 'read on nearly every cottage hearth in the manufacturing districts of south Lancashire, Leicester, Derby and Nottingham', directed his readers' attention to the 'true cause' of their sufferings—misgovernment and industrial anarchy, and its proper corrective—parliamentary reform. But the beginnings of the movement which would eventually attain these ends were marred by such events as the Peterloo Massacre of 1819 in Manchester, when a peaceful political meeting was brutally suppressed, and the passing of a number of repressive measures known collectively as the 'Six Acts'.

These events were paralleled by the intellectual activities of men as disparate as Lord Byron and William Wordsworth, Thomas Carlyle and

3

Percy Shelley, the radical poet, who viewed the coming of the machine age with fear. William Blake, who lived through the first onslaught of the industrial revolution and the Peterloo Massacre, saw mill workers as 'myriads moping in the stifling vapours' of smoke, miners as multitudes 'shut up in the solid mountains and in rocks which heaved with their torments', while munitions workers laboured like beasts and automatons, 'dishumanized men . . . scaled monsters or arm'd in iron shell Or shell of brass Or Gold'. He prophesied the misery which industrialism would bring to his fellow men, in lines which by their very familiarity helped to shape later attitudes:

> And did the countenance divine
> Shine forth upon these clouded hills,
> And was Jerusalem builded here,
> Among these dark, satanic mills?

Blake's protest in *Milton* about the 'dark satanic mills' which he felt disfigured the face of England, remains the best known of all the many expressions of distress over the effects of industrialism which occur so frequently throughout the nineteenth century.

If the machine was responsible for the decline in human and aesthetic values, then, so the argument went, it follows that a rejection of the machine, in some degree or other, could arrest this process. But the methods which were advocated took such differing forms that they are best explained by an allegory.

A painting by Walter Crane (1845–1915), *The Three Paths* of 1869, depicts an incident in a fairy story about a princess won by a prince brave enough to take the most difficult path through a wood. The suitors pause irresolutely, wondering which of the three paths to take. This image can serve as a useful visual metaphor by which to interpret three main strands in the reaction of nineteenth-century thinkers to industrialism's effect on art and life. Would-be reformers took one of three main paths. All the paths they clearly signposted with their theoretical beliefs, but unfortunately none led directly to the desired goal. Yet while all the paths frequently cross and double back on each other, it is still worthwhile to chart their course through the sombre wood of the industrial age.

The first path, figuratively speaking, led to a church. Its signpost can be imagined lettered in antique Gothic script, by A. W. N. Pugin (1812–1852). It pointed to a return to the ordered society of the middle ages dominated by the Catholic Church. While this antiquarian religious remedy could not be fully realized in Protestant England, from Pugin's work sprang the Gothic revival school of architects, whose offices between the 1860s and 1880s were the cradle and the crèche of so many of the Arts and Crafts figures whose achievements are surveyed in this work.

The second path led to a school. Its signpost, lettered in bold primary colours, was, one may imagine, the work of Owen Jones (1809–1874),

3 Walter Crane, *The Three Paths*, watercolour, signed with monogram and dated 1869 (Victoria and Albert Museum)

3

author of *The Grammar of Ornament*, one of the circle of artists and designers associated with the Victorian polymath Sir Henry Cole (1808–1882). Cole's multifarious activities, and the numerous educational institutions which he founded, were all conceived in the belief that by taking thought, and studying the finest examples of work produced in former ages, standards of industrial production and life could be improved.

The third path led to a socialist Utopia. Its signpost was lettered in the Chaucer type of Morris's Kelmscott Press. Although the most difficult path, it was also the one whose inspiration has been the most pervasive. It was forced through the thicket of nineteenth-century industrialism by John Ruskin (1819–1900) and William Morris (1834–1896), who by their teaching and example were to influence the careers and achievements of all the figures with which this book deals.

All these thinkers, however, had two ultimate and connected concerns in common; the lot of the worker and the low standards of the designs and artifacts produced by the machine. Bad working conditions, it was felt, produced bad designs. Reform working conditions and design standards would inevitably improve. The goal was the same but the means of achieving it depended on whether one's sympathy lay with the idealist school of Pugin, Ruskin and Morris or with the pragmatic approach of Cole and his circle. The problem, not surprisingly, was accentuated by the fact that each party claimed that its methods alone could achieve the desired object.

Though these concerns did not emerge as crucial issues until the middle of the century their antecedents could already be discerned in earlier years. Both the pragmatic and the Utopian approaches were clearly exemplified in the career of Robert Owen (1771–1858), who in some respects can be described as the founder of British socialism.

Owen came to London from his Welsh cottage home in 1783 at the age of 12 to work as a draper's assistant. By the age of 30 he had become manager and part owner of some large woollen mills at New Lanark, near Glasgow. A staunch democrat and genuine philanthropist, he made these mills model factories, where employees worked reasonable hours amidst pleasant and healthy surroundings for a decent living wage. New Lanark became, at a time of repressive restrictions on personal liberty, a living proof that conditions of labour could be improved without priming men to insurrection on the French Revolutionary model. But Owen's attempts during 1815–1820 to extend his experience and put it into wider practice by inducing Parliament to introduce an effective Factory Act ran counter to the repressive forces which manifested themselves in the 'Six Acts' and Peterloo. Discouraged, he sold his interests at New Lanark, and, after several fruitless attempts to establish communistic settlements in England, America and Ireland, turned his attention to the trade union and cooperative movement. His experiments, though unsuccessful, pointed many later reformers along a socialist path to a workers' Utopia.

4 Portrait of A. W. N. Pugin, aged 33, by J. R. Herbert, signed with monogram and dated 1845 (RIBA)

5 Plates from Pugin's *Contrasts*, 1834, showing modern pump and mediaeval fountain

The spiritual and aesthetic values of the Arts and Crafts movement—as compared to the secular and practical ones of Owen and his followers—owe their most distinctive debt to the influence of Augustus Welby Northmore Pugin. It is to Pugin also that the close relationship between architecture and the Arts and Crafts movement can be traced; for he saw in the comparison between the architectural purity of the mediaeval cathedrals and the monstrous effects of industrialism a paradigm of the decline towards visual and spiritual ugliness. In his book *Contrasts*, published in 1834, he draws a telling comparison between the tranquil, ordered life of the middle ages and what he felt was happening in his own time: he illustrates the free-flowing water of the mediaeval fountain and the padlocked street pump of his day, guarded by a policeman with a truncheon; the glories of the Gothic Cross at Chichester and the hideous neo-classic structure, incorporating a police station, of the modern King's Cross; almshouses and church spires in a mediaeval town replaced by factories and workhouses.

Pugin's whole life was an attempt to recapture, in his buildings, the assurance in style and way of life of the Catholic Church before the

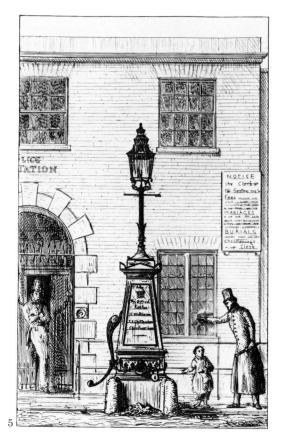

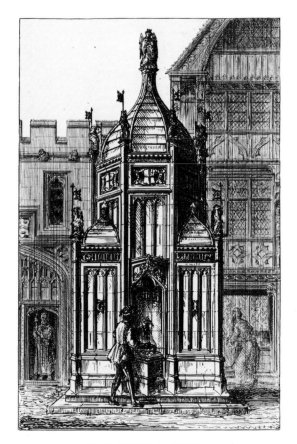

St ANNES   SOHO

CONTRASTED

PUBLIC CONDVITS

WEST CHEAP CONDVIT
THOMAS   ILAM   1479

THE SAME TOWN IN 1840

1. St Michaels Tower, rebuilt in 1750. 2. New Parsonage House & Pleasure Grounds. 3. The New Jail. 4. Gas Works. 5. Lunatic Asylum. 6. Iron Works & Ruins of St Maries Abbey. 7. St Evans Chapel. 8. Baptist Chapel. 9. Unitarian Chapel. 10. New Church. 11. New Town Hall & Concert Room. 12. Westleyan Centenary Chapel. 13. New Christian Society. 14. Quakers Meeting. 15. Socialist Hall of Science.

Catholic town in 1440.

1. St Michaels on the Hill. 2. Queens Cross. 3. St Thomas's Chapel. 4. St Maries Abbey. 5. All Saints. 6. St Johns. 7. St Peters. 8. St Alkmunds. 9. St Maries. 10. St Edmunds. 11. Grey Friars. 12. St Cuthberts. 13. Guild Hall. 14. Trinity. 15. St Olaves. 16. St Botolph.

6 Plates from Pugin's *Contrasts*, second edition, 1841, showing the same town in the middle ages and in Victorian times

7 *Labore est Orare* by J. R. Herbert, showing monks labouring in the fields with Pugin's Mount St. Bernard's Abbey in the distance (Tate Gallery)

6

7

8

8 Commemorative mosaic panel, showing Sir Henry Cole surmounted by a *maiolica* relief depicting the buildings associated with him in South Kensington (Victoria and Albert Museum)

dissolution of the monasteries. How far he succeeded can be vividly appreciated by anyone fortunate enough to visit his Mount St. Bernard's monastery in Charnwood Forest, Leicestershire, still uncannily like the peaceful scene depicted in his friend J. R. Herbert's painting of the monastery garden *Labore est Orare* (Fig. 7). Here Pugin's charismatic personality merges perfectly with the Church he loved, and a visit to it makes a moving introduction to his work. Yet his example, powerful though it was, and deeply influential on the whole Gothic revival school, was by its very Catholicism prevented from being an effective force in Protestant England.

Pugin's teachings and example were notwithstanding of seminal influence on a whole generation of architects, men like G. F. Bodley and James Brookes. They in their turn passed on to their pupils, J. D. Sedding and A. H. Mackmurdo, a sense of the Gothic tradition which in their different interpretations played so implicit a part in the ideology of the Arts and Crafts movement. As J. D. Sedding told the Art Congress in Liverpool in 1888,

We should have had no Morris, no Street, no Burges, no Shaw, no Webb, no Bodley, no Rossetti, no Burne-Jones, no Crane, but for Pugin.

Pugin's teachings were however only one of the major influences on the emergent group. Of equal importance was the emphasis on education and instruction fostered by the administrative career of that quintessential but now largely forgotten great Victorian figure, Sir Henry Cole (1808–1882). Cole created institutions with the same facility that other men write books. The Royal College of Art, the Royal School of Needlework, the Royal Albert Hall, the Public Records Office, the Victoria and Albert Museum—many of these institutions were his virtually single-handed creations, the vast and still continuing 'Open University' of Victorian England, the educational 'spin-off' from the Great Exhibition of 1851. Inseparably connected with the foundation of many of these institutions was the figure of Albert, the Prince Consort, whose fervent promotion of the arts was greatly due to Cole's encouragement.

The motive behind all these activities, so characteristically earnest and 'Victorian', was in fact closely linked to the aspirations of the Arts and Crafts movement. Cole passionately believed in good design, and held the view that it could be achieved by consulting the best precedents, the systematic study of which could add to the beauty and utility of new productions. It was for this reason that he founded museums, set up schools of design and established in 1849 the *Journal of Design and Manufacture*. The object of this periodical was to establish what its editor, Richard Redgrave, called 'sound principles of ornamental art'. The only problem was, what were 'sound principles'?

This problem of definition was clearly exemplified by what was actually produced in Cole's 'Felix Summerly Art Manufactures' venture. Cole's own attempt to establish these principles appropriately

9

9 Minton plate
commemorating the
achievements of Albert, the
Prince Consort (Victoria and
Albert Museum)

10 *Lecture to Working Men on
Ornamental Ironwork at the
South Kensington Museum*,
from the *Illustrated London
News*, March 5th, 1870

9

10

10

11

11 Teapot, cup and saucer designed by 'Felix Summerly'—Sir Henry Cole—in 1846 (Victoria and Albert Museum)

12 Cast iron doorstop designed for the Felix Summerly Art Manufactures by John Bell

took a practical form. In 1845 he had won a competition for the design of a tea service produced by Minton, using the pseudonym 'Felix Summerly'. The experience led him to believe that it would 'promote public taste' if well known artists designed articles for everyday use, so, in 1847, to further this end, he founded 'Summerly's Art Manufactures'. The enterprise lasted for about three years, until he became preoccupied with plans for the Great Exhibition, though individual firms continued to produce pieces originally designed for the venture. But, with the exception of Cole's own tea service (Fig. 11) it is difficult for us to infer from the productions of this company the principles which Richard Redgrave, Owen Jones and other artists associated with the *Journal* believed in so passionately. They abhorred exuberant and over-naturalistic patterns, carpets which suggested 'obstacles and stumbling', and china plates with embossed ornament. They anathematized tea urns with handles in the form of snakes, yet John Bell could design a door stop in the form of a three-headed Cerberus (a bull dog, a bloodhound and a deerhound). While admiring and advocating in the *Journal* patterns which were flat, 'appropriate' ornament and simple and restrained forms, Redgrave could design as a christening jug (Fig. 13) a prettily sentimental piece which gives little evidence of his practical application of these principles.

Yet for their day these ideas were both innovatory and startling. Charles Dickens, who, like Queen Victoria, can usually be relied upon to reflect popular artistic taste, equated the principles of the reformers with mechanical joylessness. In Chapter *11* of *Hard Times*, the school inspector Gradgrind, a caricature of Sir Henry Cole, says to the schoolchildren,

13 Christening mug designed
by Richard Redgrave for Felix
Summerly's Art Manufactures
in 1848 (Victoria and Albert
Museum)

You are to be in all things regulated and governed by fact. You must discard the
word Fancy altogether. You don't walk upon flowers in fact; you cannot be
allowed to walk upon flowers in carpets. You don't find that foreign birds and
butterflies come and perch upon your crockery. You must use, for all these
purposes, combinations and modifications (in primary colours) of mathematical
figures which are susceptible of proof and demonstration. This is a new
discovery. This is fact. This is taste.

The public agreed with Dickens and continued to prefer the fanciful and
elaborate ornament which the reformers condemned. At the same time
the principles of Cole and his followers were little to the taste of the
most influential of all Victorian writers on the arts, John Ruskin. It was
Ruskin who, with Pugin, laid the emotional and idealistic foundations
of the Arts and Crafts movement. Design could never be for him, as it
was for Cole, a question of adhering to rules and precedents for the
purposes of improving manufactures. For him 'the very words "School

of Design" involve the profoundest of art fallacies. Drawing may be taught by tutors, but Design only by Heaven.'

The publication of the second volume of *The Stones of Venice* in 1853 with its famous chapter on 'The Nature of Gothic' marked the most complete statement of Ruskin's views on design. It was to influence later Arts and Crafts theories more than any other work. It is a long chapter of 30,000 words, almost a book in itself. When he published it in 1892 as a separate entity, Morris wrote a preface to it, in which he said, 'in future days it will be considered as one of the very few necessary and inevitable utterances of this century . . . For the lesson which Ruskin here teaches us is that art is the expression of man's pleasure in labour.'

Ruskin's message was hammered out in memorable sentences, which still have the power to move us:

Men were not intended to work with the accuracy of tools, to be precise and perfect in all their actions. If you will have that precision out of them you must unhumanise them.

If you will make a man of the working creature you cannot make a tool. Let him but begin to imagine, to think, to try to do anything worth doing, and . . . out come all his roughness, all his incapacity . . . failure after failure . . . but out comes the whole majesty of him also.

We want one man to be always thinking, and another to be always working, and we call one man a gentleman, and the other an operative; whereas the workman ought often to be thinking, and the thinker often to be working, and both should be gentlemen, in the best sense . . . It would be well if all of us were good handicraftsmen in some kind, and the dishonour of manual labour done away with altogether. [We see] the degradation of the operative into a machine . . . It is not that men are ill fed, but that they have no pleasure in the work by which they make their bread and therefor look to wealth as the only means of pleasure.

Like all Ruskin's writings the work expressed statements of his own aesthetic preferences coupled with his social views. 'I don't care if you enjoyed it Madam, the question is, did it do you good?' he once sternly replied to a lady who had rashly said that she had enjoyed one of his lectures on design. The remark illustrates vividly the way in which for him morality was inextricably linked with the arts, which often had confusing and ambiguous results. Only the production of the work *he* liked could produce improved social conditions. 'Above all demand no refinement of execution where there is no thought, for that is slave's work, unredeemed. Rather choose rough work than smooth work so only that the practical purpose be answered, and never imagine there is reason to be proud of anything that may be accomplished by patience and sandpaper'. The rhetorical ambiguities and use of such loaded words as 'rough' and 'smooth' in such a passage, of which there are many in 'The Nature of Gothic' alienate us today, for they flaw the central message of the work.

An even more direct expression of Ruskin's social theories can be found in *Fors Clavigera*, begun in 1871. As Carlyle said in a letter to Emerson in 1872, 'there is nothing going on among us as notable to me as those fierce lightning-bolts Ruskin is desperately pouring into the black world of anarchy all round him.'

Fors Clavigera: Letters to the Workmen and Labourers of Great Britain consists of 87 letters published at monthly intervals between 1871 and 1878, and nine published between 1880 and 1884 after Ruskin's mental breakdown. Its curious Latin title, derived from Horace, can be interpreted as 'Fortune, the nail bearer', and must have been as puzzling for its proposed readers as it is enigmatic for us. In fact, it was never widely read by the labouring mass of Englishmen, but was deeply influential on the men who shaped the English Labour movement, giving British Socialism a fundamentally *moral* basis, rather than a Marxist scientific emphasis. It is Ruskin's last great work, his testament of political and social philosophy, permeated by his fanatical advocacy of a work-ethic and his dislike of the capitalist system. A capitalist lent his money to somebody else and lived in idleness on the interest, while others worked in factories. This was wrong, both for employer and for employee. Every man ought to work for his living, and preferably for some of the time with his hands. Factories really were satanic for they turned men from workers—real artisans and craftsmen—into machine minders and moreover minders of machines which always turned out nasty, inferior objects. But, he maintained, England had once been a better place than in the nineteenth century, and it could be made a better place again. The ideal socialist state he advocated would have solemn responsibilities, its first duty being 'to see that people have food, fuel, and clothes, the second that they have means of moral and intellectual education'; there would he added, be plenty of merriment: dancing, music, games.

In these letters the economic and idealistic theories advocated in those cornerstones of Arts and Crafts ideology *The Stones of Venice* and *Unto this Last* took on a new urgency. From them emerged in practical terms the foundation of the Guild of St. George, which, despite its failure, was the precursor of so many later Utopian ventures.

Funds to found the Guild were collected from 1871, but owing to various difficulties it was not licensed as a Company until 1878. The St. George's Company, as it was first called, was to embrace all those who were prepared to live the simple life, it was to reclaim barren land, its members were to contribute a tenth of their income, it was, dreamt Ruskin, 'to spread over the continent of Europe and number its members . . . by myriads'. It became, for its creator, a Tolkien-like dream of an ideal Utopia. He carried with him little squares of pure gold beaten thin, from which he meant to strike the St. George's coinage, saying, when he gave them away, 'Now you have taken St. George's money; and whether you call yourself one or no, you are a member of my Guild. I have caught you with guile!'

There is indeed something of the fairy story or pantomime about much

14 John Ruskin as 'The Realization of the Ideal' from *Vanity Fair*, 'Men of the Day', 1871

of the St. George's Guild story. Consider, for example, Ruskin's attempt to eliminate the middleman, and sell pure tea to the poor of St. Marylebone without profit. He found that 'the poor' did not like the best quality tea, and that 'the steady increase in the consumption of spirits ... slackens the demand ...'. Meanwhile 'Widow Twanky' Ruskin could not resolve the design problem of whether the sign outside the shop should be Chinese, Japanese or English in style, and 'meanwhile the business languishes ...' he wrote in *Fors Clavigera* (letter 48) which provided both a platform to promote the Guild's activities, and an account of its progress.

Ruskin's practical experiments in social philosophy to popularize the ideas of the Guild of St. George seemed doomed to failure. His ill-starred attempt in 1871 at 'keeping a bit of our London streets . . . as clean as the decks of a ship of the line' provided London briefly with the rewarding spectacle of Ruskin as crossing sweeper, but the project was soon abandoned because of mud. It was followed in 1874 by the famous Hincksey Road experiment, embarked upon while Ruskin was Slade Professor of Art at Oxford. 'I want,' he wrote to Acland in March, 1874, 'to show my Oxford drawing class my notion of what a country road should be . . . I want to level one or two bits . . . and sow the banks with wild flowers . . . and to let my pupils feel the pleasures of *useful* muscular work'. Downes, Ruskin's head gardener, supervized the work, and among the diggers were Toynbee, the future historian, and Oscar Wilde.

Predictably the Guild of St. George's practical achievements were negligible and widely scattered—the acquisition by gift of three acres of moorland at Barmouth in Wales, a commune of agriculturalists on fourteen acres near Sheffield, the revival of the Langdale linen industry, and a wool mill at Laxey in the Isle of Man.*

Ruskin's Guild of St. George used up all his energies, depleted his finances, and bored his friends. Yet its influence was remarkable, for from it sprang the later Guilds of the 1880s. But Ruskin's teachings found even more fruitful soil. They proved the seminal influence for William Morris, whose career unites virtually all the idealistic and practical aims of his predecessors. It was his achievements and example, more than any other factor, which led to the emergence of the Arts and Crafts Movement, and the part he played in this process must be examined at length.

*By 1884 the membership of the Guild stood at 57, and although surprisingly it survives today its activities are now chiefly connected with the supervision of the Ruskin Museum collections now at Reading University.

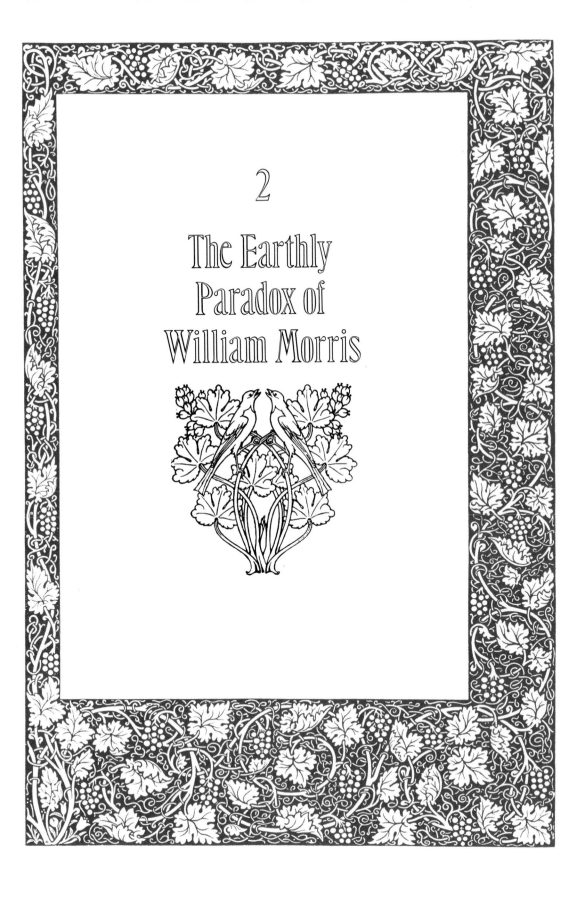

2

The Earthly Paradox of William Morris

N 1857, William Morris, then a young man of 23, took part in that most rumbustious of Pre-Raphaelite escapades, the painting of the Oxford Union frescoes, which depicted episodes in the story of King Arthur and the Knights of the Round Table. Characteristically, he felt strongly that he could not hope to paint knights in armour unless he had experienced the feeling of wearing armour, and he had a helmet and suit of chain mail 'run-up' to his own design by a surprised Oxford blacksmith. To the delight of his friends he insisted on wearing the suit to a dinner party and succeeded in getting his head stuck in the helmet.

This story inevitably reminds us of Cervantes' Don Quixote. But Morris was far more than a tilter at windmills or an 'idle singer of an empty day', as he described himself. Even this comic antiquarian escapade reveals his energetic determination to succeed in what he described as 'the necessary ordinary details' of any craft process which he revived. Significantly his own fresco in the Oxford Union scheme was the first to be completed, and he then turned his attention to painting a decorative pattern on the roof beams of the building which remains one of the most striking features of that remarkable, and still little visited, room interior.

A few years later, in 1861, the firm of Morris, Marshall, Faulkner & Company, Fine Art Workmen in Painting, Carving and Furniture and the Metals, was founded. The aims of this firm, from which Morris and Company was later to emerge, were set forth in a prospectus, or rather a manifesto. In the light of later developments, this was a surprising document, and is worth quoting extensively:

The growth of Decorative Art in this country, owing to the efforts of English Architects, has now reached a point at which it seems desirable that Artists of reputation should devote their time to it . . . Up to this time, the want of that artistic supervision, which can alone bring about harmony between the various parts of a successful work, has been increased by the necessarily excessive outlay, consequent on taking one individual artist from his pictorial labours.

The artists whose names appear above hope by association to do away with this difficulty . . . they will be able to undertake any species of decoration, mural or otherwise, from pictures, properly so called, down to the consideration of the smallest work susceptible of art beauty . . . They have therefore now established themselves as a firm, for the production, by themselves and under their supervision, of—

1. Mural Decoration, either in Pictures or in Pattern Work, or merely in the arrangement of Colours, as applied to dwelling-houses, churches, or public buildings.

2. Carving generally, as applied to Architecture.

3. Stained Glass, especially with reference to its harmony with Mural Decoration.

4. Metal Work in all its branches, including Jewellery.

5. Furniture, either depending for its beauty on its own design, on the application of materials hitherto overlooked, or on its conjunction with Figure

and Pattern Painting. Under this head is included Embroidery of all kinds, Stamped Leather, and ornamental work in other such materials, besides every article necessary for domestic use.

What makes this document so surprising in view of Morris's later stress on the value of individual executant craftsmanship, is the condescending tone adopted towards the 'Fine Art Workmen' who by their 'artistic supervision' could transform 'the smallest work susceptible of art beauty'. J. Mackail, Morris's biographer, was probably right in ascribing the authorship of this prospectus to the 'imperious accent' of Rossetti rather than Morris, although initially Morris shared their views, as can be seen from his own painted decorations on the cabinet by Webb of 1862 (Fig. 15). Later, however, he came to repudiate the implications present in the statement of the original ideas of the firm in favour of a more soundly based craft aesthetic. The general public were less quick to change their attitudes, and the emphasis was to remain on the value of 'art' rather than 'craft' until the 1880s. 'You know, I wouldn't mind a lad being a cabinet maker if only he made Art furniture', once remarked a lady to Morris.

Morris's personal contributions may have helped involuntarily to perpetuate these attitudes, for they were all essentially two-dimensional and pictorial: stained glass, chintzes, tapestries, wall-

15 Cabinet of mahogany and pinewood on stand, designed by Philip Webb in 1861. The front is painted by William Morris with scenes from the life of St. George (Victoria and Albert Museum)

paper, books, illuminated manuscripts, all extensions in one way or another of his consummate gifts as a pattern maker. The three-dimensional crafts of furniture, glass and metalwork were the responsibility of others in 'the Firm'—at first of Maddox Brown, the elder statesman of both the Pre-Raphaelite Brotherhood and the Morris Company, and later of Philip Webb, the architect of Morris's home, the Red House, and George Jack, an American (1855–1932).

The link between architecture and the Arts and Crafts movement was a strong one. Morris and Webb had met in the office of the Gothic revival architect George Edmund Street (1824–1881), a place which turned out to be a nursery of the Arts and Crafts movement. Edmund and John Dando Sedding were there for some years; Webb came as Chief Assistant in 1852, Morris spent a short time there as an articled pupil, Norman Shaw followed Webb. The pattern of Webb's life and career establishes a classic prototype to be followed by many subsequent figures in the Arts and Crafts movement. Like him they would train initially as architects, but find the discipline of producing designs on paper for translation into bricks, mortar and drains by other hands unfulfilling. This experience was vividly described by Webb when his pupil W. R. Lethaby asked him why Morris had abandoned architecture. Webb replied, 'Because he found he could not get into close contact with it; it had to be done at second hand.' The desire to get closer to the actual process of creation, the thrill of seeing an artifact growing under their hands, was to become an impulse shared in common by men

16 Morris's 'Daisy' wallpaper of 1862—one of the first productions of Morris, Marshall, Faulker & Company, in 1862 (Victoria and Albert Museum)

17 Oak table designed by Philip Webb (Victoria and Albert Museum)

17

18 Walter Crane's *Tea at the Red House* (Fine Art Society) depicts an idyllic scene with maids carrying trays out onto the lawn. But the life of a servant to Morris could be arduous. One of his maids at his later home, Kelmscott House, has recorded how as a young girl of twelve she had to stay up until two in the morning to tend the fire while Morris and his friends discussed socialism

as diverse as Mackmurdo, Ashbee, Gimson and Henry Wilson. Like Webb they were led from architecture to the crafts, in an inexorable pattern that is one of the most recurrent features of the movement. The architectural offices of the Gothic and Queen Anne revivals 'begat' the Arts and Crafts movement. In 1875 Morris reorganized the firm on far more practical business lines than the early happy-go-lucky enterprise. At this period, significantly, he produced a number of highly successful designs for machine-made carpets, a fact which clearly contradicts the familiar and widely accepted over-simplification of Morris's teachings which states baldly that he completely repudiated machine production. As he himself wrote, 'men should be masters of their machines, and not their slaves as they are now'.

In 1881 the firm was successfully established at Merton , and from its workshops emerged the well known chintzes, wallpapers, woven wool tissues and tapestries, the wool for which was washed in the waters of the river Wandle and dyed on the premises. 'He actually did create new colours', wrote a pupil of his, 'in his amethysts and golds and greens; they were different to anything I have ever seen; he used to get a marvellous play of colour into them. The amethyst had flushings of red; and his gold (one special sort), when spread out in the large rich hanks, looked like a sunset sky . . . when he ceased to dye with his own hands I soon felt the difference. The colours themselves became perfectly level, and had a monotonous prosy look; the very lustre of the silk was less beautiful. When I complained, he said "Yes, they have grown too clever at it—of course it means they don't love colour, or they would do it".'

19 William Morris's works at
Merton. Watercolour by L. L.
Pocock 1850–1919 (Victoria
and Albert Museum)

20 William Morris's
'Carnation' chintz of 1875
(Victoria and Albert Museum)

21 'Peacock and Dragon',
woven wool tissue, 1878,
designed by William Morris
(Victoria and Albert Museum)

22 Washing wool in the river
Wandle at Merton, from a
Morris & Co Catalogue, 1910
(William Morris Gallery)

23 Dying wool in the vats at
Merton, from a Morris & Co
Catalogue, 1910 (William
Morris Gallery)

This remark reveals the perfectionist discontent that so characterizes Morris. The financial and artistic success of his company would have been enough to satisfy any other designer or genius. But Morris was cast on a heroic scale. The very success of his business ventures, and the demand for his fabrics and other productions began to anger and frustrate him, since the inevitable high costs of manufacture led to their being extremely expensive, prompting him to ask despairingly, 'Why should I minister to the swinish luxury of the rich?' At first he found relief from this dilemma by organizing the Society for the Preservation of Ancient Buildings, and by lecturing on the techniques and artistic problems of the crafts which he had so successfully revived. In a delightful caricature by Sir Edward Burne-Jones we see him in action, a dynamo of energy, buttons about to fly in every direction, seated at the loom giving a lecture on weaving to an amazed audience, a scene which recalls his pungent words that, 'if a man can't write an epic poem while weaving a tapestry there's not much in him!'

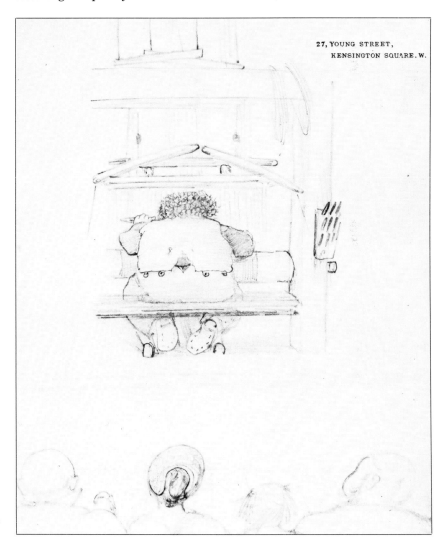

27, YOUNG STREET,
KENSINGTON SQUARE. W.

24 Morris lecturing on weaving. Cartoon by Sir Edward Burne-Jones (William Morris Gallery)

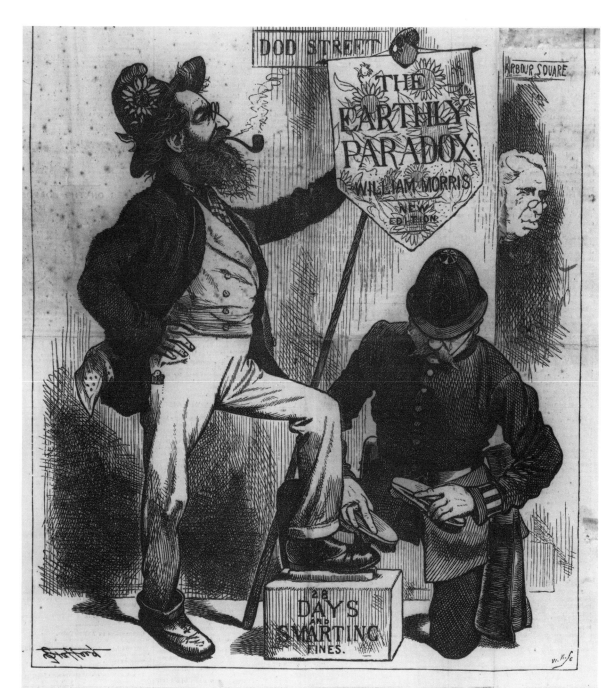

THE ATTITUDE OF THE POLICE.

(DEDICATED TO "THE FORCE," MR. SAUNDERS, AND THE SOCIALISTS.)

25 Morris the campaigner as
'the Earthly Paradox'.
Cartoon from *Fun*, 1888
(William Morris Gallery)

The steady development of Morris's socialist views accentuated his feelings of discontent. He came to believe implicitly that progress in the arts could not be achieved under a capitalist system, and he threw his energies into the heady but disillusioning world of active political agitation, speaking up and down the country, founding the Socialist League in 1885, and editing the magazine *The Commonweal.* But even for an idealist on the epic scale of Morris, platform experience led to the development of a pragmatic grasp of political realities. He became increasingly sceptical about the feasibility of any individual attempt to reform art and society that fell short of the complete overthrow of the capitalist system. This belief accounts for his gruff and deprecating reactions to the Utopian schemes propounded by the young designers who, fired by the inspiration of his lectures, came to regard him as a father figure. Morris's relationship with this younger generation of disciples are of particular importance, and can best be described by examining his contact with one man in detail, rather than by generalizations. The ideal figure for this role is provided not by relatively well known men like Mackmurdo and Ashbee, but by the complex and intriguing personality of the man who first joined the words 'arts' and 'crafts', T. J. Cobden-Sanderson (1840–1922), bookbinder and printer.

As a young man Sanderson prayed successfully 'Sweet God, souse me in literature', though he left Cambridge without taking a degree. He tried various occupations, and for a time studied medicine. In 1871 he was called to the bar, but practised with little enthusiasm until in 1881 his health broke down. While in Italy recovering he met and fell in love with the daughter of Richard Cobden the politician and famous radical speaker on the Corn Laws issue of the 1840s, and, when he married her, he characteristically prefixed her surname to his own. At his wife's wish, shortly after their marriage in 1882, he abandoned the bar in order to seek self-expression in the work of his hands.

Thus his career as a bookbinder began, at the advanced age of 43, on the 24th June, 1883. We are able to date the event so precisely because of an entry in his journal, which describes a supper party with William and Jane Morris. 'I was talking to Mrs Morris after supper, and saying how anxious I was to use my hands—"Then why don't you learn bookbinding?" she said. "That would add an art to our little community, and we would work together". "I should like", she continued, "to do some little embroideries for books, and I would do so for you". Shall bookbinding, then, be my trade?'. Jane Morris rarely spoke, virtually her only other recorded remark being one made to Bernard Shaw, on giving him a second helping of pudding: 'That will do you good: there is suet in it', but her conversation with Cobden-Sanderson certainly produced results.

Her suggestion fell on ground already prepared, both by the example of her husband's work and lectures, and by the influential teachings of John Ruskin. This inspiration and teaching led directly to the Idealism (with a capital I) with which Cobden-Sanderson approached both book

THE IDEAL BOOK OR BOOK BEAUTIFUL The Ideal Book
is a composite thing made up of many parts & may be
made beautiful by the beauty of each of its parts—its
literary content, its material or materials, its writing or
printing, its illumination or illustration, its binding &
decoration—of each of its parts in subordination to the
whole which collectively they constitute: or it may be
made beautiful by the supreme beauty of one or more
of its parts, all the other parts subordinating or even
effacing themselves for the sake of this one or more, &
each in turn being capable of playing this supreme part
and each in its own peculiar and characteristic way.
On the other hand each contributory craft may usurp
the functions of the rest & of the whole and growing
beautiful beyond all bounds ruin for its own the common cause. I propose in this brief essay, putting aside
for the moment the material, paper or vellum, the binding & decoration, & the literary content of the Book
Beautiful, to say a few words on the artistic treatment
of the vehicle of expression—Calligraphy, Printing, &
Illustration—and on the Book Beautiful as a whole.

CALLIGRAPHY

HANDWRITING and hand decoration of letter &
page are at the root of the Book Beautiful, are at the
root of Typography & of woodcut or engraved Decoration, & every printer, & indeed every one having to
do with the making of books should ground himself
in the practice or knowledge of the Art of Beautiful

26 'The Ideal Book' by T. J.
Cobden-Sanderson

production and book binding. His activities reflect in one craft the
attitude of a whole generation of earnest young men who came to see in
craftsmanship and a simple life style a Utopian escape route from the
restrictive pressures of the late Victorian age. Cobden-Sanderson,
besmocked, bereted, bow-tied and bearded, the Utopian Craftsman
personified, speaks for them all when he writes: 'The higher aim is to
dignify labour in all the lower crafts, to induce men of education to
follow in the same direction, and so to lift all the arts and crafts, upon
which life rests, by the spirit in which they are performed, to consecrate
the arts and crafts to the well being of society as a whole . . .' and so on in
even more exalted Ruskinian strains.

This lofty idealism was, somewhat surprisingly, not altogether to the
taste of the founding father of the movement, William Morris. On 21st
March, 1885, Cobden-Sanderson records, 'Morris called on Thursday,
and we lunched together at Rules. He began a talk about my prices.

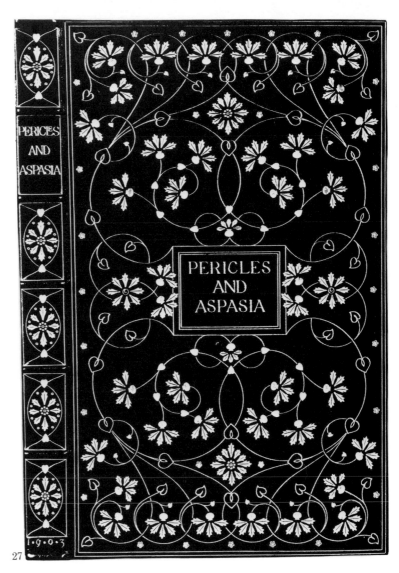

27

27 Binding for Landor's
Pericles and Aspasia executed
by T. J. Cobden-Sanderson at
the Doves Bindery in 1904
(Victoria and Albert Museum)

28 Photograph of Cobden-
Sanderson from *The
Craftsman*

Premised that "People would go to the cheapest market", and almost as
though he approved; thought my work too costly; book-binding should
be "rough"; did not want to multiply the minor arts(!); went so far as to
suggest that some machinery should be invented to bind books.

"The cheapest market!" Should I then go to the sweaters in the East
End, and there buy my shirts and clothing?'

How extraordinary are these remarks of Morris! They seem to express
the exact antithesis of all he has come to represent for us, and our
sympathy for the perplexed Cobden-Sanderson deepens when we recall
an earlier entry in his journal on 21st July, 1882: 'I have been reading
Morris's *Lectures on Art*: I read the first "On the Lesser Arts". It
inspired me again with ardour, and made my own projected handicraft
seem beautiful to me.'

How could Morris of all men thus turn like Doctor Frankenstein to
destroy his own creation? Such a paradox demands explanation.

29 The Cobden-Sandersons'
home, from *The English
Illustrated Magazine*, 1891

Bookbinding, more than any other craft, summarizes perfectly the
essence of the philosophy of hand, as opposed to machine, production.
Yet a book bound by hand with the utmost skill and aesthetic sensitivity
produces two sharply opposed reactions. At one and the same time it
arouses deep admiration for its beauty and an irrational irritation. Why
expend so much energy and skill on binding the pages of a text which
thus becomes too precious to handle, but can only be genuflected to
through the anathema of a glass-fronted bookcase? While the opposite
aesthetic arguments justifying the craft will readily spring to mind, it
perfectly illustrates a process which, to adapt Oscar Wilde, may be
described as 'Craft for Craft's Sake', and recalls also his aphoristic
correction to Ruskin and Morris: 'All Art is entirely useless.'

For Morris, in 1885, actively involved in politics, the printing press
and the book were primarily tools with which to influence the masses,
rather than the artistic vehicle they were to become for him six years
later when he founded the Kelmscott Press. In the mid-1880s he was still too
involved in politics to view with much sympathy either the aesthetic
agonizings of Cobden-Sanderson, or the Guild schemes of A. H.
Mackmurdo or C. R. Ashbee. Both men experienced 'dissillusioning
douches of cold water', to use Ashbee's phrase, when explaining their
ideas to Morris.

30 Morris cutting a wood block for *The Earthly Paradise*, by Sir Edward Burne-Jones, from *The Collected Works of William Morris* (original drawing in the British Museum)

KELMSCOTT PRESS, UPPER MALL, HAMMERSMITH.

March 31st, 1894.

This is the Golden type.

This is the Troy type.

This is the Chaucer type.

Halliday Sparling, 8, Hammersmith Terrace, London, W., to whom should be addressed all inquiries as to books to which no publisher's name is attached.

31 Colophon of the Kelmscott Press (William Morris Gallery)

These concerns also explain why Morris, although always regarded with the utmost respect by the younger men of the Arts and Crafts movement, played only a relatively minor part in the genesis of the annual exhibition which formed the public platform from which they strove to convert the public to their ideals. This idea had been gestating for many years, for the supremacy of the Royal Academy, and the over-rigid distinction between fine and applied arts, proved increasingly irksome to men nurtured by the writings of Ruskin. He it was who, writing to Morris in 1878, had first suggested, 'How much good might be done by the establishment of an exhibition, anywhere, in which the right doing, instead of the clever doing, of all that men know how to do, should be the test of acceptance.'

This aim, ten years later, after several years of ventilation in the correspondence columns of *The Times*, the traditional escape valve of the English intelligentsia, had become realizable. In 1887 a group of deocrative designers, notably Walter Crane, W. A. S. Benson, William De Morgan, W. R. Lethaby, Lewis F. Day and Heywood Sumner, circulated a scheme for an exhibition to be held the following year. The initial clumsy title of 'The Combined Arts' was changed by Cobden-Sanderson into the refined battle cry of 'The Arts and Crafts Exhibition Society'. Morris, although so much the 'onlie begetter' of the whole concept, had several practical reservations. On 31st December, 1887, he wrote: 'One thing will have to be made clear, i.e. who is to find the money . . . the general public don't give a damn about the arts and crafts, and our customers can come to our shops to look at our kind of goods, and the other kind of exhibits would be some of Walter Crane's works and one or two of Burne-Jones: these would be the things worth looking at: the rest would be of an amateur nature, I fear.'

This fear of amateurism arose from the activities of the various associations which had sprung up in the 1880s under the name of Home Arts, Cottage Art Societies or Village Industries, all directly or indirectly the result of the impact of Ruskin's teachings on well intentioned philanthropic patrons. For Morris, with his innate professionalism, these activities seemed merely to play with more radical problems. He also found the Arts and Crafts Society's avowed aim of crediting the name of the executant workman of an individual piece, as well as the designer, a trivial one, for it was not by printing lists of names in a catalogue that the status of the workman as a class could be raised.

Yet despite his lukewarm enthusiasm for the first public manifestation of the movement with which his name is so closely associated, it is undoubtedly true that all its members would have proclaimed that the example of Morris was one of the main determinant factors in their lives and choice of careers. Indeed Ernest Gimson, described by Pevsner as the greatest English artist craftsman, was virtually launched on his path through life by an early meeting with Morris. It is, however, worth pointing out some equally potent, although less obvious elements in the intellectual yeast that led to the rise of this generation of craftsmen.

The essays of Ralph Waldo Emerson, the poetry of Walt Whitman, and Henry Thoreau's *Walden* may seem too far removed from the problems of industrial late 19th-century England to have much relevance. Yet lines such as Whitman's moving idealization of the joiner and mason in the 'Song of the Broad Axe' from *Leaves of Grass* added a new dimension of humane optimism to the thought of some young Englishmen of the 1880s, men like A. H. Mackmurdo and C. R. Ashbee, so aware of the clashing dichotomies of the familiar arguments over industrialism that had raged in England since the beginning of the nineteenth century:

The house builder at work in cities or anywhere
The hoist up of beams, the push of them in their places, laying them regular,
Setting the studs in their tenons in the mortices according as they were prepared,
. . . The blows of mallets and hammers, the attitudes of the men, their curv'd limbs . . .
The crowded line of masons . . . the continual click of the trowels striking the bricks
The bricks one after another laid so workmanlike in its place, and set with a knock of the trowel-handle . . .
. . . The shapes arise!
The shape measur'd, saw'd, jack'd, stain'd
. . . The shape of the little trough, the shape of the rockers beneath the shape of the baby's cradle.
    The shapes arise
Shapes of doors giving many exits and entrances
The door that admits good news and bad news.

Whitman's poetry, the more meaningful since it had been written while the poet supported himself as a carpenter, and the inspiring advocacy of the simple self-sufficieny of rural life in Thoreau's *Walden*, first published in England in 1884, gave a new impetus to a generation of individualists seeking, like Thoreau, 'a broad margin' to their lives. Despite Thoreau's distrust of possessions, and preference for nature ('You may melt your metals and cast them into the most beautiful moulds you can; they will never excite me like the forms which this molten earth flows out into . . .') the emergent Arts and Crafts movement derived from his book a sense of priorities: 'The cart before the horse is neither beautiful nor useful. Before we can adorn our houses with beautiful objects the walls must be stripped, and beautiful housekeeping and beautiful living be laid for a foundation: now, a taste for the beautiful is most cultivated out of doors, where there is no house and no housekeeper'. Like him, believing that 'men have become the tools of their tools', they attempted to establish their own individual Utopias.

C. R. Ashbee, looking back in 1917, in a work entitled significantly

e Metal Shops, Campden

32 The Metal-working shop at Chipping Campden, woodcut by E. H. New from C. R. Ashbee's *Craftsmanship in Competitive Industry*

Where the Great City Stands—a quotation from Whitman—posed these issues succinctly:

With the coming of mechanical power and the displacement of the hand by the machine, the conditions of human life were changed—the home and women's portion in it, the man's labour, his relation to society, his conception of right and wrong. The history of every country for a thousand years has no fact so important as the change from domestic to factory industry. The disappearance of the small workshop with the guild system that regulated human labour and set its standard of quality in life and work of man's hands, is more far-reaching than any religious or dynastic change. But the Arts and Crafts Movement made the discovery that it was only in the small hand workshop that those things could be had again for which that movement stood.

The first of these attempts to recapture the cohesion of the Guild system in a small workshop, was to be Arthur Heygate Mackmurdo's Century Guild venture.

3
Arthur Heygate Mackmurdo
and the
Century Guild

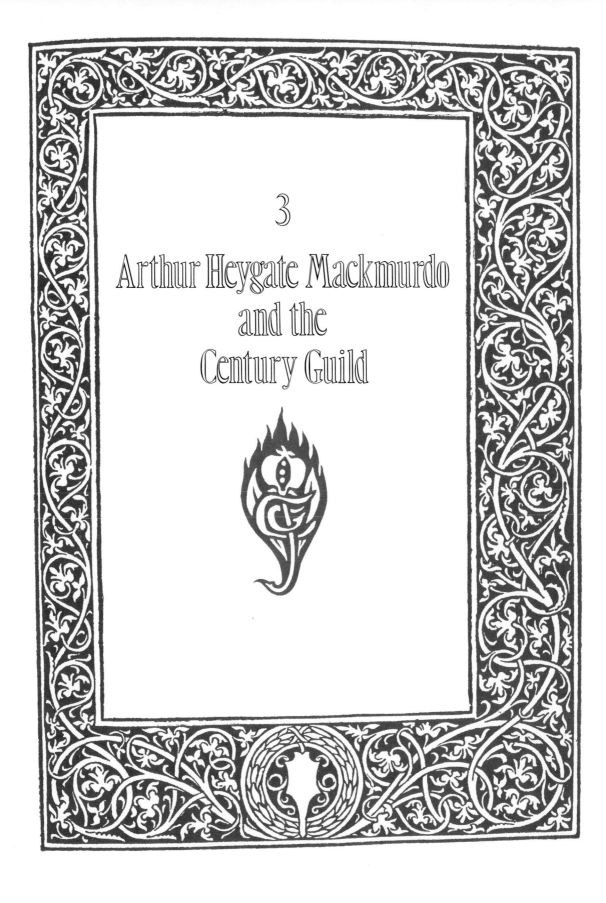

I N THE RICH archives of the William Morris Gallery, Walthamstow, a letter from Mackmurdo to his niece Elinor Pugh, dated 7th April, 1938, describes a visit to his house in Essex of the brilliant young German scholar Nikolaus Pevsner. Mackmurdo writes, 'I was so thoroughly vivisected there was no part of me which had not been cut up, pulled to pieces, and thrust under his microscopic eye'. Mackmurdo, then aged 86, felt a certain flattered if puzzled surprise that his activities over half a century earlier in forming the Century Guild should attract such detailed investigation, while his later economic and monetary theories, published with such titles as *The Human Hive* (1926) should merit less attention. It is possible to feel deep sympathy with Mackmurdo in his predicament. Like Henri Van de Velde (1863–1957) whose later years were also spent in the Proustian revival of *Memories of Past Times* he had lived a long time, and his career had had many facets, yet in old age belated recognition was focused chiefly on the work of his youth.

Almost certainly he would have disapproved of his posthumous fame as the great precursor of the Art Nouveau style. Just as Rachmaninov fled with horror from the sound of the constant reiteration of his over-popularized *Prelude in C sharp minor*, the constant reproduction in

33 Caricature of A. H. Mackmurdo riding a hobby horse, from 'Arthur, Hys Boke', a satire by his niece Elinor Pugh, 1905

didde he acquaintance manie friends and some of th ese frendys didde gather unto hym and so didde he and th ey make another and littler Guild and the syne of this littler Guild was an horse the reason whereof shall be told. Now Arthur and his frendys said to themselvys We are al le yclothed in shertes of linen blue and breche of yellow yette ys there more to doe so that our solempne and grete fraternitie maye be well observed. We have each one his own peculiar hobby horse and hym will we generally ryde and eke carry a sunflower in our handys and whenne ye one of us sh all paynte a missal or an other shalle endite a rhym e or another shalle doe any other thing after hys fashion thenne shall alle ye othren be hys herauldes and so loud yell and crie hys praizes ye endilong daye that alle ye citie may hear and be astonied at findynge so grete an artist in theire midst. So whensoever they had finish ed their several workes so didde they stamp it and mark

34 Frontispiece from *Wren's City Churches* by A. H. Mackmurdo, 1883

every work on Art Nouveau of the title page of his book, *Wren's City Churches*, published in 1883, would baffle and perplex him. It was, he said to his friend Sir Henry Sirr, a book of which 'he was far from proud . . . conscious that he erred in the style of writing, and [he] dismissed mention of it'. The book remains a historic curiosity, for there can surely be no work less read for its content and best known for the very dissonance of its title page from its subject. In this, it typifies the complex ambivalence of Mackmurdo's achievement, for his Century Guild is of equal importance, not only for its anticipation of Art Nouveau, but as a seminal influence on the nascent Arts and Crafts movement.

Arthur Heygate Mackmurdo was born, symbolically, in 1851, the year of the Great Exhibition. 'My father', he relates in his unpublished notes for an autobiography* 'was practically interested in science, and my mother was genuinely interested in the art movement leading up to the 1851 Exhibition of Mechanics, Science and Art—the absorbing influence at the period when the die of my life was cast: Not allowed to read till I was seven, I found my delight in building structures with wooden bricks of which I had a generous collection.' One cannot help wondering if his bricks included some of the terracotta examples designed by Henry Cole for children, and brought out by Minton's, for the Felix Summerly Art Manufactures venture. It would have been extremely appropriate if they had been, for Mackmurdo's later architectural work was to develop the same feeling for abstract form that was admired if not practised by the Cole circle. Mackmurdo's father, a wealthy chemical manufacturer, moved in intellectual circles. 'My character', Mackmurdo continues, 'was accentuated and influenced in adolescence by those with whom I was brought into personal contact. Thomas Carlyle, Herbert Spencer, John Ruskin and James Brookes.' Mackmurdo met Brookes after he had decided at the age of eighteen to become an architect and been apprenticed to the unimpressive T. Chatfield Clarke, from whom he felt he learnt nothing of architecture or art. Brookes (1825–1901), a Gothic Revival architect of the generation of Bodley and Street, was to remedy these omissions. Mackmurdo writes:

He was essentially a craftsman. His hesitation in taking me into his workshop was due to the sense that as a craftsman he must do every bit of work with his own hand. Accordingly, every detail of his buildings exhibited feeling, thought and action. It was this that fascinated me and made his buildings so impressive . . . He designed not only the general plan and structure, but every detail to door hinge and prayerbook marker. When he consented to take me I had to do the same after an apprenticeship in tracing his drawings. I then saw how the powerful expression of his building was due to the personal touch in every detail of a perfectly co-ordinated Conception. His difficulty [was] in getting the work executed in days when there were no craftsmen . . .

*Now in the William Morris Gallery, Walthamstow.

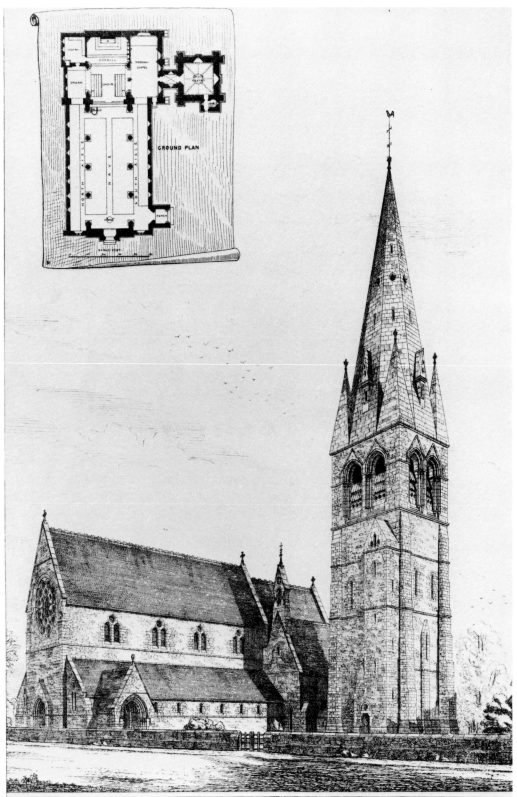

Church:of:the:Annunciation:Prick:End:Chislehurst: James:Brooks:Architect.

Mackmurdo continues:

Then I came under the influence of and into personal contact with John Ruskin and Robert Browning. The analytical mind of the former, the sympathetic mind of the latter led me into new mental excursions. I travelled Italy and France with Ruskin and under his direction made graphic studies of stones, insects, plants, mountains and buildings from barns to cathedrals, by which I had a grounding in the laws underlying all organic forms. But previously to this I attended the Lambeth drawing school, drawing the figure from life ... The Human form became to me the type of Beauty in its divinity of Structure and Expression ... This pattern ... must be the pattern for all human creations. All this naturally led me to a review of Art generally; also to an impulse to express my feelings in a more spontaneous method than Architecture permitted. I was drawn into decorative design ...

Mackmurdo's own words need little amplification. It is interesting to see in this account of his early development the use of the word 'organic', for it is just this appreciation of the growth of natural forms which gives his later asymmetric designs their power. During his walking tours with Ruskin in 1874, Mackmurdo also became deeply impressed by Italian Renaissance architecture, an appreciation which later developed into his admiration for the classical architecture of Wren. It is the alternate play of these different impulses which gives Mackmurdo's Century Guild work its rich complexity and fascination.

In 1875 Mackmurdo set up a practice as an architect, first at 28, Southampton Street, and after 1880 at 20, Fitzroy Street, London. The house was arranged as a sort of bachelor's club, for Mackmurdo did a great deal of entertaining and was extremely hospitable. By his mother, whose maiden name was Carte, he was related to Rupert D'Oyly Carte, founder of the Savoy Operas, and Mackmurdo moved freely among the social lions of the aesthetic period. He wrote of Whistler, in a letter to Nikolaus Pevsner,

I first knew [him], meeting him at RDC's as near as I can remember about 1876–80. He and Wilde were often asked there to supper, amusing RDC. They were the two best talkers in London ... Whistler persuaded RDC to make his drawing room at Adelphi Terrace a harmony in yellow. He painted the grand piano an old gold colour with traces here and there of complementary greys and greens ... When Whistler had his one man show of paintings I helped him in arranging his attractive schemes. Drawings hung in white frames on white walls; floor covered in white matting. The slightest touches of colour in a drawing shone out and caught the eye at once.

These exciting contacts must have increased Mackmurdo's desire to enter the field of the decorative arts. He resolved to train himself in various craft techniques:

I schooled myself in the techniques of modelling and carving, trying my hand at some ornamental stonework for the first house I built. I learnt to do repoussé

35 Church of the Annunciation, Prick End, Chiselhurst by James Brooks, from *The British Architect*

39

work in brass . . . and embroidery. Under a skilled carpenter I learned enough about materials and constructive processes to design pieces of furniture . . . While I agreed with Morris that the unrestrained use of machinery would kill every attempt to rescusitate Art and Beauty, I still clung to the hem of his garment, and did such architectural and craft work as I could . . . Wallpapers, cretonnes, room fabrics, brass and iron work, furniture of all descriptions. I gathered round me a number of artists and craftsmen who could supply all that was required for the decorations, furnishings and equipment of a house. I called the group the Century Guild.

The Century Guild, founded in 1882, had as its aims 'to render all branches the sphere no longer of the tradesman, but of the artist', and to 'restore building, decoration, glass painting, pottery, wood-carving and metal to their rightful places besides painting and sculpture'. Yet while its name reflects the Ruskinian credo, and its manifesto the work of

36 'Blackbird' design for wallpaper by Herbert Horne, *c.* 1883 (Victoria and Albert Museum)

40

Morris and Company, the group's work was to develop on very different lines. With the exception of William De Morgan, who was associated with the Guild as a tile designer, the members were young and unknown men. Selwyn Image (1849–1930), the co-founder, had met Mackmurdo when, as a young clergyman, he had studied drawing with Ruskin at Oxford. His growing interest in pottery and the arts led him to resign Holy Orders in 1883 when embarking on the Guild venture, but his religious training enabled him to specialize in designing stained glass and ecclesiastical embroidery, while also working in other decorative fields. Herbert Horne (1864–1916) joined Mackmurdo as an apprentice after two years in a surveyor's office. He was only eighteen, but already capable of producing wallpaper designs of great power and also designs for metalwork. It was probably through Horne's deep interest in the history of art that the Century Guild magazine, the *Hobby Horse*, took on its role as precursor of *The Burlington Magazine*. This interest later

37 'Tulip' design for wallpaper by Herbert Horne, *c.* 1883 (Victoria and Albert Museum)

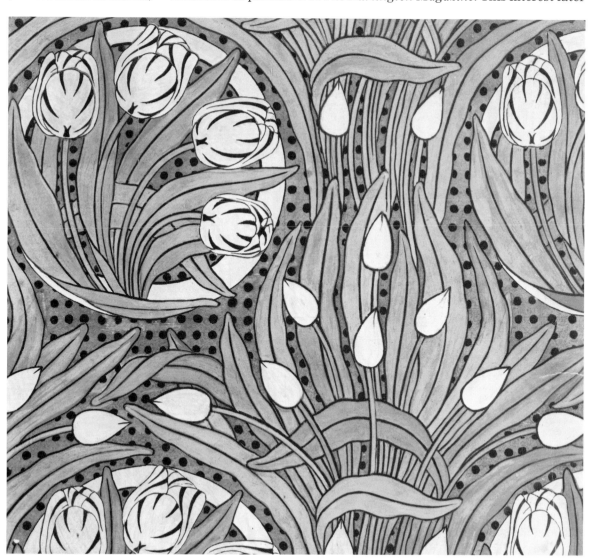

made Horne an inspired collector, at first of English watercolours, and later of the work of the Italian Renaissance, in which field he became a leading authority, anticipating Berenson. Other members of the Guild included the metalworker Clement Heaton, son of the founder of Heaton, Butler and Bayne, stained glass manufacturers, and Benjamin Creswick, who had taught himself sculpture while working in a Sheffield knife factory.

The Century Guild's work was from the first of remarkable diversity. Perhaps its most famous single product, because of its anticipation of Art Nouveau sinuosity, was the celebrated chair of 1883 with its elaborate fretwork back, possibly inspired by the borders of one of William Blake's *Songs of Innocence*, for an article on Blake by Gilchrist

38 Chair designed by A. H. Mackmurdo and probably made by Collinson and Locke, *c.* 1883. The exuberant fretwork decoration which often enlivens the sobriety of Mackmurdo's furniture is entirely derived from seventeenth-century prototypes (Rev. W. Roberts)

39 Detail, showing the fretwork back of the Mackmurdo chair

39

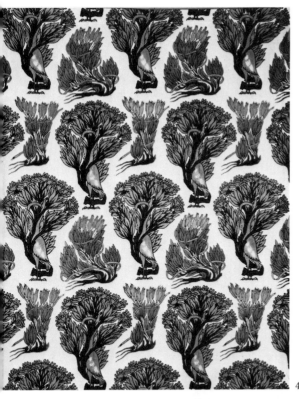

40 'Bird and Tree', printed
cotton design by A. H.
Mackmurdo, *c.* 1884. Probably
printed by Simpson and
Godlee (Victoria and Albert
Museum)

41 'Cromer Bird', printed
cotton designed by A. H.
Mackmurdo, *c.* 1884. Probably
printed by Simpson and
Godlee (Victoria and Albert
Museum)

42 Settle designed by A. H.
Mackmurdo and made by
Collinson and Locke, *c.* 1886.
The fabric of the curtains is
an angel and trumpet design
by Herbert Horne, and the
brass panels are by Bernard
Creswick. This was almost
certainly designed for Pownall
Hall, Cheshire (Victoria and
Albert Museum)

appeared in an early number of the *Hobby Horse*. The same frond-like curves appear in designs for printed fabrics like the 'Bird and Tree', and the 'Cromer Bird' by A. H. Mackmurdo, and the swirling thorn background to the Angel and Trumpet design of Selwyn Image used to upholster a settle. (See Figs. 40–42). Flickering upwards, flame-like movement features appropriately in the embroidered fire screen (Fig. 43), while branch-like forms in iron spread themselves across the solid door of Pownhall Hall in Cheshire, restored for Henry Boddington by the Century Guild in 1886 (Fig. 44). These asymmetrical patterns contrast with the bold, simple forms of the furniture, and in particular with the writing desk of 1886, with its distinctive geometric finials, the thumbprint of Mackmurdo's architectural style (illustrated in Fig. 45).

43 Fire screen in satinwood with panels embroidered in silks and golden thread, designed by A. H. Mackmurdo in 1884 (William Morris Gallery)

44 Front door at Pownall Hall, Cheshire, decorated with Century Guild ironwork, 1884 (photograph by Richard Sword)

43

45 Writing table designed by
A. H. Mackmurdo in 1886
(William Morris Gallery)

46 Century Guild stand at the
1886 International Exhibition,
Liverpool, from *The British
Architect*, 1886

This finial became one of his favourite devices, occurring again and again in the design both of permanent furniture and the temporary structures of trade stands at exhibitions like the 1886 Liverpool International Exhibition. C. F. A. Voysey (1857–1941) whose furniture stylistically was greatly influenced by Mackmurdo, and who was a peripheral associate of the group, surprisingly does not mention this in a letter to Mackmurdo of 1930, in which he does say, 'You were a very great influence in those days and set me going on wallpapers and fabrics'. It is tempting to see this influence in such examples as the 'Merle' pattern of ten years later (Fig. 50) although of course Voysey was too individual a designer to be described as purely derivative.

47 C. F. A. Voysey, sideboard, 1900 (Victoria and Albert Museum)

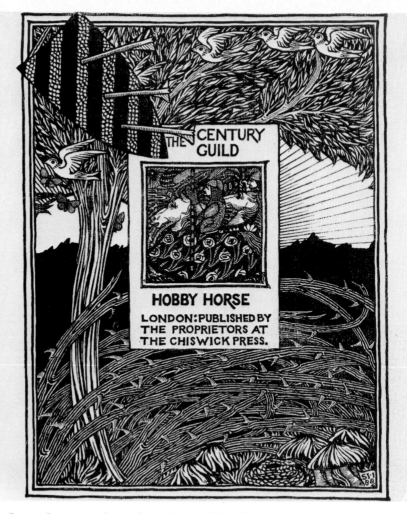

48 Cover of the Century Guild *Hobby Horse*, Volume 1, 1886

49 Woodcut tailpieces from The *Hobby Horse*, by A. H. Mackmurdo, Selwyn Image and Herbert Horne

It was however through its journal the *Hobby Horse* that the Century Guild achieved its greatest influence, for its production heralded the birth of a whole series of illustrated periodicals in the 'eighties and 'nineties. A notable feature of the magazine was its embellishment with small wood block cuts by Herbert Horne, Selwyn Image and A. H. Mackmurdo which make it one of the most handsomely produced of all periodicals. Mackmurdo's words summarize its importance: 'The variety of contributors and the range of art covered may be gathered from the following names from the list of contributors—Ford Madox Ford, William Strang, William Bell Scott, Ruskin, W. M. Rossetti, Christina Rossetti, Oscar Wilde, Frederick Shields, Simeon Solomon, G. F. Watts, E. Burne-Jones, Matthew Arnold, J. Addington Symonds, Arthur Symons, W. B. Yeats, Wilfred Scawen Blunt, etc.' The list is striking evidence that Mackmurdo's social gifts must have been considerable. It takes an editor of real genius and humanity to include talent both in the ascendant like Oscar Wilde's, and in the descendant, like Simeon Solomon's. But the most important effect produced by the publication of the periodical was the part it played in influencing

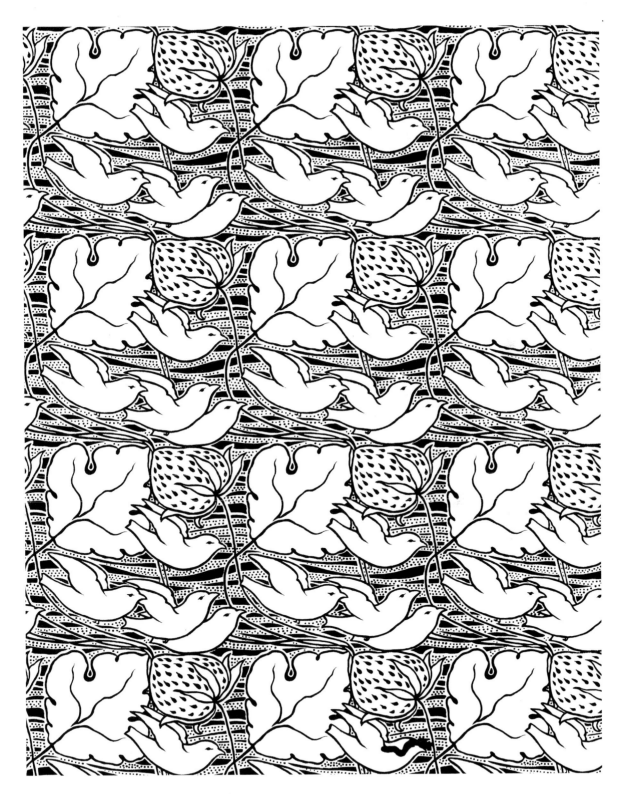

50 C. F. A. Voysey's 'Merle'
wallpaper, 1901 (Victoria and
Albert Museum)

William Morris's decision to found the Kelmscott Press. Mackmurdo writes:

For one of his unbounded energy the range of crafts which, in 1888, he [Morris] was then practising in such accomplished manner would be, one would have thought, sufficiently engaging. But it was not so. I well remember at this time showing him a number of the *Hobby Horse*, the magazine of the Century Guild which I had established—and telling him of the difficulties one had to overcome in getting a page of printed text that was a pleasure to look at. What art there was in proportioning its mass; in setting this text with nicely proportioned margins upon the page, in the spacing of letters and of lines; in the choice of ink, of paper, and above all of available type. The sight of the poor best that by painstaking and taste had been achieved with such material as one had then had, fired Morris with enthusiasm. He instantly saw what could be done. 'Here is a new craft to conquer and to perfect. A new English type needs to be founded'. He then and there resolved to master the situation by setting up a press of his own.

51 Printing the Kelmscott Chaucer (Fulham Public Libraries)

it with an horse's head for that folken should know it to be ye handiwork of theire fraternitie Now Arthur and ye other brethren of ye Guild of ye horse did dwelle in a fayre mansion in ye citie and ye doores thereof were shinynge white like unto a lake at dawn. And they said unto themselues "Before alle thynges let us be geuere in oure furniture and ye appurtenances thereof for if we have curtayns and cushions and chaires of ease then will menne see that we are but as ye common run of people and so that they shall think us as gods or as ye special chosen and only true Administrators of the great Goddess Culture" so will we sup offnuts and crushed wheat serued on a table all bare of linnen clothe and other frippery and in each room will we haue straight chaires

52 Caricature of A. H. Mackmurdo from 'Arthur Hys Boke' by Elinor Pugh, 1905 (William Morris Gallery)

The subsequent founding of the Kelmscott Press, and the development of the whole private press movement, in many ways the most successful of all Arts and Crafts productions, can thus, to a large extent, be said to stem from the example provided by the *Hobby Horse* magazine.

In her amusing spoof illuminated manuscript *Arthur hys boke* (Fig. 52) produced in 1905, Elinor Pugh, Mackmurdo's niece, described his motives in disbanding the Century Guild in 1888 as being bored with having hair upon his shoulder. Although facetious, this suggestion has more than a vestige of truth in it. For Mackmurdo the Century Guild had been a youthful interlude in which he could put Ruskinian theories into practice.

For some years he turned his attention solely to his architectural practice, playing an important part in the building of the Savoy Hotel, and producing a number of remarkable buildings, including a coldstore, a public house and a gymnasium, of which the best surviving example is probably a large house, 25, Cadogan Gardens, built in 1899 for Mortimer Mempes, Whistler's disciple, an exciting blend of Mackmurdo's admiration for Wren and his passion for vertical features. 'But', he writes, 'more and more I was conscious of an influence drawing me aside from architecture and planning of buildings to study problems connected with the Social Structure . . .'

Just after his partner Herbert Horne's departure from the practice in 1900 to settle in Florence to pursue his career as an art historian, commemorated in the bequest of his house, the Museo Horne, to that city on his death in 1916, Mackmurdo also decided to abandon architecture and devote himself to monetary reform. He built himself a large house, Great Ruffins, at Wickham Bishops in Essex, symbolically surmounting it with a large tower to enable him to gaze at the stars. Unfortunately, soon after its completion, financial pressures forced him to sell the house, and he moved to a smaller house nearby, occasionally persuading the new owner to organize large parties when his old urge for social gatherings grew too strong. Increasingly he turned to economic research, publishing *The Human Hive, Its Life and Law* in 1926, and *A People's Charter* in 1933. He died in 1942 at the age of ninety-one.

Sixty years had elapsed since, at the age of thirty-one, he had founded the Century Guild, and in six years, Janus like, played a major formative role in the genesis both of Art Nouveau, the Arts and Crafts movement, and the typographical revolution that developed into the Private Press movement. Such achievements, progressive and influential, had gained from the first international recognition, and continue to merit the utmost respect. Their sheer variety demands explanation, and accounts for the motivation that led Pevsner to place Mackmurdo under the microscope to our lasting benefit. But despite the abandonment of these activities for the sociological work to which he attached greater importance, the old 'master builder' gazing at the stars, the quintessential Utopian craftsman, is the image by which he would, perhaps, wish to be remembered.

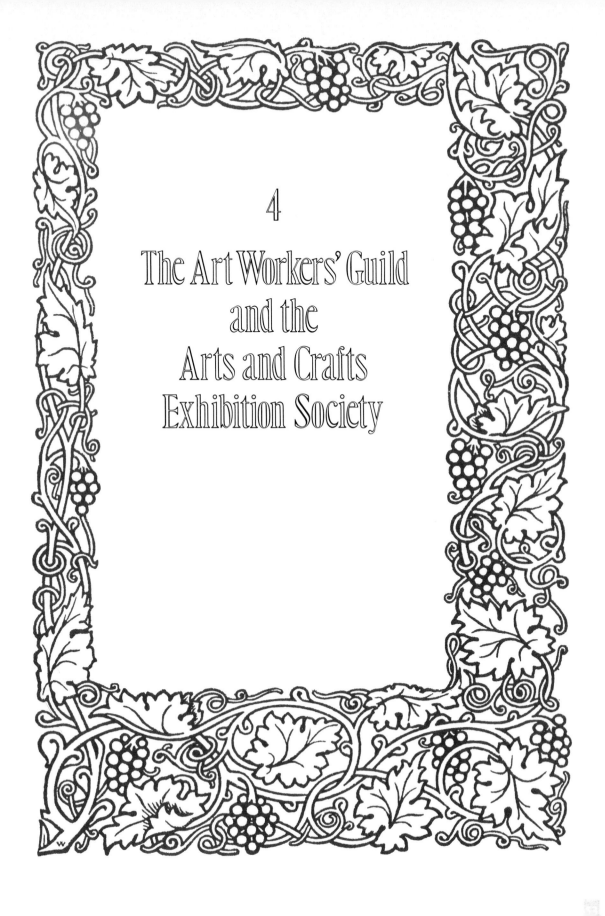

4

The Art Workers' Guild
and the
Arts and Crafts
Exhibition Society

HE CRADLE and the creche of many of the most active Arts and Crafts infants were the offices of the Gothic Revival architects of the 1860s, 1870s and 1880s, men like G. E. Street, James Brooks, G. F. Bodley, J. P. Seddon, Norman Shaw and J. D. Sedding. Amongst these architects raged learned arguments over the relative purity of different phases of the Gothic style. From this schooling in eclectic borrowings from the Early English and Perpendicular periods emerged a generation of young men who had absorbed solid architectural knowledge which was to give their work its formal strength. Their practical experience as architectural assistants of contracting out jobs to building specialists had given them their initial introduction to individual crafts, often to become their major interests.

It is illuminating to eavesdrop on one of the most important of their mentors, exchanging views with another teacher on the principles which should be instilled in their charges. Here is Norman Shaw writing to John Dando Sedding in 1882:

Look at the enclosed photo. And say if it is not *copied* (and I use the word advisedly) I don't mean imitated—but clean copied from old work—general design and detail down to the smallest cusp. It is possible that this can be *great* Art—I fear not—and yet it is a good work of Bodley's; a man we both sincerely admire . . .

Can good 19th-century work done by educated and intelligent mortals consist in a servile copy of the 15th century? Real work of any kind whether good or indifferent must I contend be *living* work. Our art is like a language; it must be either living or dead. What I complain of is—that there is absolutely no idea in such a thing as that screen. It is simply . . . a clean copy. Of course all this is very dreadful—and though we are talking of Bodley we are all in the same boat.

In this passage Shaw shows his awareness of the dangers of too slavish an adherence to the Gothic style. His own advocacy of a vigorous classical eclecticism deriving from Wren, was to become best known through the satirical lines of W. S. Gilbert, 'Convince them if you can— That the reign of good Queen Anne was culture's palmiest day'.

These famous lines from *Patience*, first performed in 1881, were prompted by the aesthetic elysium of Bedford Park, the west London suburb developed in the 1870s and 1880s by a shrewd property dealer with artistic interests, J. Comyns Carr. His architects, E. W. Godwin, and even more Norman Shaw, providing in the suburb a quaintly olde worlde Queen Anne village setting ideal for those aesthetically aware middle class intellectuals who sought an escape from the commercialism of London life. In the words of one of the many satirical poems on the suburb, 'they could sit and read Rossetti there by a Japanesy lamp', or slip across to the stores or the Tabard Inn for refreshment when tired of cultivating sunflowers in their back gardens. In the evenings they could pass a convivial hour in the Clubhouse or take part in the amateur dramatic productions of great originality put on by the community. On Sundays they could worship in the sage green

53 Allegorical design for the
Arts and Crafts Exhibition
Society by Walter Crane
(Victoria and Albert Museum)

54 Front elevation for the
Tabard Inn and stores at
Bedford Park by Norman
Shaw (Victoria and Albert
Museum)

55 A back garden in Bedford
Park with St. Michael's
Church in the background,
from a coloured lithograph by
T. Hamilton Jackson, 1881
(Victoria and Albert Museum)

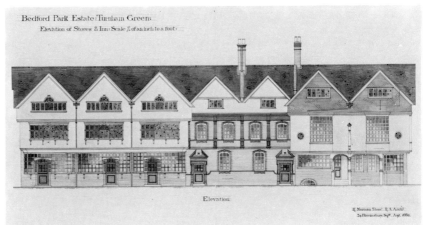

54

interior of Shaw's St. Michael's church. Bedford Park has a surprising significance in an Arts and Crafts context, for in a curious way it reflects some of the main concerns of the movement—the ideal of a community life, and a concern for design, so readily distorted into a subject for parody seized upon with delight by pens as diverse as those of George du Maurier and G. K. Chesterton.

The 'Queen Anne' tag was always to remain attached to Norman Shaw, despite the originality of some of his later work. John Dando Sedding (1838–1891), however, remained faithful to the Gothic revival principles which he and Shaw had absorbed when both men were articled to G. E. Street in the late 1850s. Sedding was reinforced in these views by his friendship with Ruskin in the 1870s and by his deep admiration for William Morris. Sedding's brief career was to include the design of embroidery, wallpapers and church metalwork, and the creation of the most moving of all Arts and Crafts churches, Holy Trinity, Sloane Street, a serenely elegant witness to all that the movement could at its best achieve. From Sedding's office emerged Henry Wilson (1864–1934) his chief assistant who succeeded to his practice and carried through many of the projects left uncompleted at his death. Wilson, and John Paul Cooper (1869–1933), another Sedding pupil, both took up metalwork as incidental to their architectural practice, but later made it their main interest. Other pupils included Ernest Gimson and Ernest Barnsley, whose brother Sidney was articled to Norman Shaw, working under the supervision of William Richard Lethaby (1857–1931), who was chief assistant to Shaw from 1881 to 1893.

All these young men came into close contact with Philip Webb, the elder statesman of the Morris firm, and a close friend of Shaw and Sedding. From him they acquired his own individual credo. 'Architecture to Webb', to use the words of his biographer W. R. Lethaby, 'was first of all a common tradition of honest building. The great architectures of the past had been noble customary ways of building, naturally developed by the craftsmen engaged in the actual works. Building is a folk art, and all art to Webb meant folk expression embodied and expanding in the several mediums of different materials.'

While all these figures were to make important individual contributions to the movement, Wilson, and even more Lethaby, were to emerge not merely as craftsmen and teachers, but as leaders. Leadership is a quality that both invites and defies analysis, particularly when discussing the foundation of artistic groups. Yet while difficult to define, its presence can be readily recognized, and certain individuals seem to possess an almost uncanny power of uniting into a coherent organism a disparate group of highly individual figures. Lethaby's, and to a lesser extent Wilson's, influence is a recurrent thread in the complex warp and woof of the movement's development from the 1880s to the first world war.

Their role as leaders arose naturally from their senior position in the offices of Shaw and Sedding, which in 1883 became Utopian forums of debate on the future role of the decorative arts in society. The personnel of both offices were fired with indignation at the Cinderella role of the applied arts in its relationship to those ugly sisters of the Architectural and Fine Art establishment, the Institute of British Architects and the Royal Academy. Monthly meetings were held near the Bloomsbury church, St. George's, from which the group took its name, for despite the similarity of title it had no connection with Ruskin's Guild of St. George. Encouraged by Norman Shaw, the group gained many important adherents. In January, 1884, at a meeting held at the Charing Cross Hotel, it fused with a vocal côterie of intellectuals, 'the Fifteen', which had been in loose association for four years, under the leadership of Lewis F. Day (1845–1910). Day had started his own business in 1870, designing stained glass, textiles, wallpapers, embroidery, carpets,

56 'Appleblossom' wallpaper by Lewis F. Day, printed by Jeffrey & Co for W. B. Simpson, 1880–1885 (Victoria and Albert Museum)

57 'The Goose Girl' design for
tiles by Walter Crane, 1880
(Victoria and Albert Museum)

pottery and book covers, both achieving commercial success and
becoming a respected critic. Prominent among his adherents were
Heywood Sumner (1853–1940), who specialized in *sgraffito* ecclesiastical decorations and embroidery; Henry Holiday (1839–1927), stained
glass designer and dress reformer; T. M. Rooke (1842–1942), Burne-
Jones' chief studio assistant, and Hugh Stannus, who was the friend
and biographer of Alfred Stevens. But the most important member of the
group was Walter Crane (1845–1915), whose success as an illustrator of
children's books, and designer in all aspects of the decorative arts,
played a major part in shaping the aesthetic tastes of the time. A
committed socialist, Crane was a natural leader for a movement
committed to radical change in the status of the applied arts.

These highly individual, often diametrically opposed thinkers
became the founder members of the Art Workers' Guild. It is hardly
surprising that from its outset such an amorphous group should take on
a non-activist role, perhaps best described by Henry Wilson when
Master of the Guild in 1917, who said it formed 'a spiritual oasis in the
wilderness of modern life'. This escapist role was not, however, purely
passive. Meetings of the Guild afforded the designers and theoreticians
of the 1880s and subsequent decades the ideal opportunity to meet, and
the successful cross-pollination of ideas led to the emergence of a
generation of teachers of remarkable distinction whose influence is still
felt today in the Colleges of Art whose traditions they did so much to
establish. The Art Workers' Guild, formed largely by men born in the
1860s and brought up in the shadow of High Victorian South Kensington, was united, both 'creators' and 'teachers' alike, by a burning sense
of educational mission. Indeed, eventually membership of the Guild,
which was by election among its members, was itself to become a
powerful qualification for those applying for high positions in art
administration.

But in 1884 all this lay in the future. What was urgently needed, it was
felt by many members of the Guild, was a more publicity-conscious
approach, a public platform on which not only their ideals, but their
work itself could gain wider recognition. Indeed, one of the main planks
in the programme of the St. George's Art Group had been the
promulgation of an active exhibition society, and it had been hoped by
many that the Art Worker's Guild would fulfill this function. As it did
not, a faction of activists arose in 1886, prominent among them being
W. R. Lethaby, Lewis F. Day, T. J. Cobden-Sanderson, Heywood
Sumner, William De Morgan, Walter Crane and W. A. S. Benson
(1854–1924), metal worker and friend of Morris and Burne-Jones. It
was Benson who became the actual catalyst, in 1888, of a scheme for an
exhibition under the title of 'The Combined Arts'.

The change of title to the 'Arts and Crafts Exhibition Society' has
become history. The first exhibition was held at the New Gallery, in the
autumn of 1888, then an avant-garde setting for such events as the first
appearance, a few years later, of Isadora Duncan before a London

Yᵉ GOOSE GIRL

·O·WIND·BLOW·CONRAD'S·HAT·AWAY;
·AND·MAKE·HIM·FOLLOW·AS·IT·FLIES;
·WHILE·I·WITH·MY·GOLD·HAIR·WILL·PLAY;
·AND·BIND·IT·VP·IN·SEEMLY·WISE;

60

58 William De Morgan's favourite pot, seen in his hands in the portrait below (Victoria and Albert Museum)

audience. Writing in 1916, on the occasion of the exhibition at the Royal Academy, which can be seen with hindsight to have been the apotheosis of the Society's activities, Julia Cartwright reminisced vividly about the first show:

> ... when the New Gallery opened its doors, a thrill of pleasure and surprise ran through the spectators. Many of us remember the beautiful effect of the Central Court—the pyramid of De Morgan tiles glowing with the ruby lustre of old Gubbio ware, with Persian and Rhodian blues, Mr Benson's luminous copper fountain, Mr Sumner's sgraffito designs and gesso roundels, the glorious tapestries from Merton Abbey, and all the lovely colour and pattern in silk embroideries and exquisitely tooled morocco, that met the eye. Even wall papers might become things of beauty, we felt, when we saw the joy of the springtime reflected in Walter Crane's design 'Under the Greenwood Tree' and 'The Golden Age' return in his embossed leather of silver and gold. There were greater treasures too—cartoons by Burne-Jones for those stained glass windows which are the glory of St. Philip's, Birmingham ...

The exhibition's success can be gauged by an address made a few weeks after it opened in Liverpool at the first congress of the National Association for the Advancement of Art and its Application to Industry. The speaker was, surprisingly, Lord Leighton, doubling as President of the Congress and the Royal Academy. With his customary urbane circumlocution he praised the exhibition and admitted that the men by whom it was promoted had already done much to improve and elevate the taste of the community. Walter Crane, who, with Morris, Day, and Cobden-Sanderson also read papers at the Congress, ironically thanked Leighton for 'at least the verbal recognition extended to the Arts and Crafts of design and the claim of those who work in them to the title of artists', and suggested that the Academy should lend its noble galleries to the next Society show. This was, he knew, an unlikely contingency, for the Liverpool Congress was but another well intentioned opportunity for the promotion of familiar and high-principled hot air, although some of the views put forward at it, and the later Congresses at Edinburgh and Birmingham, have, with hindsight, a radical novelty.

59 Portrait of William De Morgan by Evelyn De Morgan (De Morgan Foundation)

But rather than digress to discuss these mainly fruitless attempts to find the path to the promised land, it is more rewarding to survey, in some detail, the gradual change in the exhibits at the Arts and Crafts shows, which continued to be held at the New Gallery until 1910. It is possible by studying the catalogues to trace the arrival of successive generations of innovators and craftsmen, and the growth of the individual influence of teachers at Schools of Art and organizers of Craft Guilds. Most of the works illustrated in this chapter were first seen either at New Gallery shows or at the numerous emulative exhibitions held up and down the country.

The first show was, as already mentioned, dominated by the work of William De Morgan, who was then at the height of his powers as a brilliant ceramic decorator and tile designer. De Morgan, a close associate of both Morris and Mackmurdo, had experimented for years with lustre glazes which were inspired by his love of Isnik pottery of which he had made a deep study at South Kensington, as the Victoria and Albert Museum was then known. His highly original imagination, which at the end of his life was to bring him belated fame as a novelist and led him to be hailed as a second Dickens for such novels as *Joseph Vance*, found its visual expression in the grotesque 'Beasties' which form such a distinctive feature of his tile designs. He also delighted in the design of ship panels based on the prototype of classical triremes, and stylized flower designs. Such tiles were particularly admired by William Morris who recommended their use to clients, and shared with De Morgan a dream of tile-clad houses which could be hosed down, thus combating the pollution of sulphurous London fogs. Number 8, Addison Road, the home of Charles Debenham, a great patron of the Arts and Crafts movement, was designed by Halsey Ricardo in a manner which put this idea into practical form. It provides to this day a striking testimony of the outstanding achievements of De Morgan as a tile designer, and also contains some fine mosaics by Gaetano Meo, another exhibitor at the first exhibition, an Italian who had started his career as an artist's model.

Morris and Company were of course much in evidence at the first show, with work ranging from the 'Woodpecker' tapestry, now at the William Morris Gallery, to 'Hammersmith' rugs. Morris himself

60 'Hammersmith' rug
designed by William Morris
(Victoria and Albert Museum)

61 Panel of nine tiles by
William De Morgan (Victoria
and Albert Museum)

exhibited some pages of his illuminated version of the *Rubaiyat of Omar Khayam*.

Other prominent features of the exhibition were wallpapers by Crane, the President ('The House that Jack Built'), J. D. Sedding (the 'Westminster' and 'Jacobean') and Lewis F. Day.

The Century Guild were also extensively represented by a wide range of their productions, including a number of plaster reliefs by Benjamin Creswick and a series of initial letters for the *Hobby Horse* by Herbert Horne. The Guild and School of Handicrafts, which had not yet become an independent entity, made its appearance as the Toynbee Hall School and Guild of Handicraft.

But perhaps the most striking new work was provided by the exhibits of W. A. S. Benson, who also wrote an expository article on metalwork for the catalogue, in which he states, 'There can be no doubt that the extent of the existing disassociation of the producing craftsman from the consumer is an evil for the arts, and that the growing preponderance of great stores is inimical to excellence of workmanship . . . the position of the village smith plying his calling in face of his customers might not suit every craft, but the services of the middleman are dearly bought at the price of artistic freedom . . . The more ordinary wares have all life and feeling taken out of them by mechanical finish, an abrasive process being employed to remove every sign of tool marks. The all important surface is thus obliterated'. Benson's words possess a prophetic irony.

62 Initial letters for the *Hobby Horse* magazine designed by Herbert Horne

63

63 Teapot, coffee pots and jug
by W. A. S. Benson in copper
and silver plated nickel,
between 1895 and 1900
(Victoria and Albert Museum)

64 Silver kettle on a stand by
W. A. S. Benson, 1913 (Fine
Art Society)

64

Less than twenty years later Liberty and Company's 'Tudric' and
'Cymric' cast metalwork was to be given careful distressing to produce a
'hand-beaten' effect, much to the wrath of C. R. Ashbee. This revolution
in public taste, reflected in such commercial activity, is an eloquent
testimony to the influence of Benson and other metal-workers who set
up their own workshops in the 1880s and 1890s. Benson's achievement
was, however, to differ from that of his contemporaries, for he was able to
make a happier liaison than most between the exigencies of commercial
machine techniques and handcraftsmanship. His earliest ambition had
been to be an engineer, but after an academic education he had
compromised by founding, in 1880, a small workshop, encouraged by
William Morris. In 1887 he built a factory in Hammersmith, and opened
a retail shop in Bond Street. His productions, whether tea-services,
vases, kettles and stands have a bold innovative quality which can be
seen at its most original in his lamps, gas and electric light fittings, with
their effective and remarkably advanced reflectors.

65 Two vases from the
Sunflower pottery at Clevedon
by Sir Edward Elton (Victoria
and Albert Museum)

66 Copper jug made at the
Keswick School of Industrial
Art (William Morris Gallery)

67 Brass kettle on stand made
at the Keswick School of
Industrial Art, *c.* 1900 (Fine
Art Society)

65

66

67

66

The second exhibition in 1889 proved still more successful, to the delight of Morris, who wrote gleefully to Jane to tell her that in the first three days the visitors numbered twice as many as in the previous year. The exhibition continued to show the supremacy of Morris's influence, an essay by him on the art of dyeing appearing in the catalogue, and the Galleries becoming the crowded venue for the delivery of his famous lecture on Gothic Architecture. Lectures on aspects of individual crafts by their practitioners were a regular feature of all the exhibitions, attracting great public interest. Among the innovations at the second exhibition was a case of pottery produced by Sir Edmund Elton at the Sunflower pottery at his family home at Clevedon in Somerset, simple shapes decorated with coloured slip of purple, violet, green and grey colours, with flowers and snakes modelled in relief applied to the surface of the vessels, and covered with a transparent glaze. There were also some fine pieces by Mark V. Marshall, one of the most imaginative potters in the Doulton studio.

Among the more interesting metalwork on show were some pieces produced by the Keswick School of Industrial Art,* founded in 1884 by Canon and Mrs. Rawnsley as an evening institute. By 1898 it was to become a full-time institution through the success of its productions, which were sold, along with the productions of other rural schools, through the Home Arts and Industries Association and the Rural Industries Co-operation Society who had a retail shop in Bond Street.

*Still active today as the Keswick Industrial Arts.

68 Vase, covered jar and jug, 1899, 1898, 1897. Della Robbia Pottery, Birkenhead (the Williamson Art Gallery and Museum, Birkenhead)

68

69 Clutha glass designed by Christopher Dresser (Victoria and Albert Museum)

One of its early full-time directors was to be Harold Rathbone the founder of the Della Robbia pottery at Birkenhead.

The third exhibition in 1890, the last of the annual exhibitions, was less successful, perhaps because its exhibits now lacked the impact of novelty, and also because a number of items on display had just that quality of amateurism which Morris had feared would appear. There were, for instance far too many, to adapt a phrase immortalized by Cicely Courtenidge, 'double dozens of dainty decorative dessert doylies', and works with titles like *The Pixies Ride*, exhibited by the Editor of *Home Art Work*, not to mention a grandfather clock case in burnt wood engraving, shown by the Working Ladies Guild, and a linen border for draping an easel, 'copied from old work' and shown by the Ladies Art Work Depot. Walter Crane, also, had one of his less successful allegorical works on view, an Irish National Banner, emblazoned with Irish emblems, the motto 'Children of the Gael Shoulder to Shoulder', and the autograph of Charles Stewart Parnell, the Irish leader.

There were, of course, many exhibits of fine quality, notably some 'Clutha' glass designed by Dr. Christopher Dresser, and made by J. Couper, and Sons. 'Clutha' (old Scots for 'cloudy') glass was coloured green, amber and clouded yellow with variegated streaks and bubbles, sometimes with patches of aventurnine. Its shapes, of great originality, were derived from natural forms and Egyptian and Persian models. Produced in Glasgow from 1885 to 1905, its designs were the work of both Dresser and George Walton (1867–1933), a contemporary of Mackintosh and also a fine designer of furniture.

Several cases of Barum ware pottery were shown by C. Brannam (1855–1937) of Barnstaple. This ware, which was later extensively marketed by Liberty and Company, comprised vases and jugs of simple form with moulded decoration and painted designs of marine and animal life in muted greens, blues and yellows. Liberty and Company itself was represented by a mantel fitting and two fireside chairs by L. F. Wyburd, their chief furniture designer, an early indication of what was to become a long-standing close relationship between the firm and the Arts and Crafts movement. In the next twenty years Liberty's and Heal's were to make the products of the group not only widely available, but also fashionable, a process not without its ironies and anomalies.

Another name later to become very familiar in the Society's catalogues also appears for the first time, that of Ernest Gimson, exhibiting somewhat surprisingly a sampler, embroidered by Phyllis Lovibond. The design has a *faux-naif* quality which, while extremely representative of the mood of this exhibition, was very different from his later robust pattern making.

70 Barum ware by C. Brannam (Victoria and Albert Museum)

71 George Walton, stained oak chair used in the Cranstone Tea Rooms, Glasgow (Fine Art Society)

69

72 Peitschenhieb embroidery
by Hermann Obrist
(Munchner Stadt Museum,
Munich)

The mixed quality of this exhibition led the Society to decide that in future shows should only be held at three-yearly intervals. Surprisingly, virtually the only important foreign exhibitor during the 1890s, the decade which saw the great flowering of Art Nouveau on the continent, was the German designer Hermann Obrist (1863–1927). Obrist had dedicated himself to the applied arts in 1882, founding an embroidery studio in Florence in 1892, which he moved to Munich two years later. It comes as something of a shock to find his name featuring in the 1896 Arts and Crafts Exhibition with no less than nine exhibits, for his name has come to be regarded as almost synonymous with the 'whiplash' line of the art nouveau style at its most extreme, the adjective indeed being derived from one of his most famous embroideries, *Peitschenhieb*. These exotic intrusions apart, the walls of the Society's exhibitions remained relatively unsullied from what its President, Walter Crane, denounced as, 'that strange decorative disease known as *L'Art Nouveau*', although it was felt that constant vigilance was necessary to keep its infectious and pernicious influence at bay, both in the exhibitions and in the Colleges of Art from which came so many of the exhibits.

The success of the Arts and Crafts Exhibition Society's London shows led to the growth of a number of other Exhibition Societies and Guilds throughout the country. The standard of work at many of these shows was, as Morris had feared, of an amateur nature, but this was by no means invariably the case. The Women's Guild of Binders, for example,

73, 74, 75 Bindings by the
Women's Guild of Binders,
1899–1902 (Victoria and Albert
Museum)

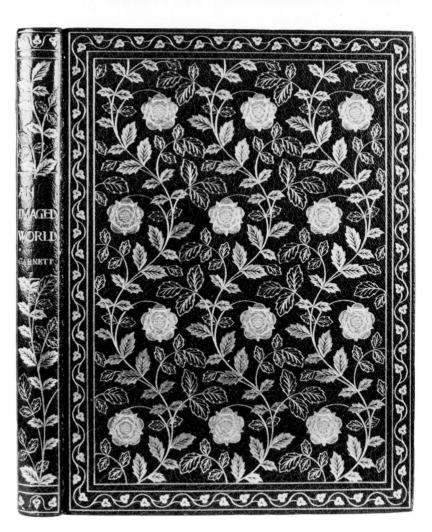

76 A binding by the Women's
Guild of Binders (Victoria and
Albert Museum)

which profited from the inspirational example of Cobden-Sanderson, produced many bindings of high quality.* But while it is fascinating to examine, in reviews in *The Studio*, the changing pattern of the exhibitions year by year, enough has been said to suggest their heterogeneous nature, and it is more profitable to examine the emergence of some inspirational teachers of the crafts in the more important Colleges of Art, notably in Birmingham, Glasgow, and the Central School of Arts and Crafts in London.

*For a full discussion of their work, see Anthea Callen, *Angel in the Studio*, chapter 7.

5

The Teaching Dilemma:
Art versus Craft

HE GOVERNMENT SCHOOL of Design, established in 1837, was not a success. It lacked direction and a sense of purpose, and aroused irritation in the manufacturers it was designed to help. But it did employ one designer of great though flawed genius. Alfred Stevens (1817–1875) was appointed Assistant Master at the Government School of Design at Somerset House in 1845.

Born at Blandford Forum in Dorset he had studied art for ten years in Italy on funds raised by friends, including a year spent in Thorwaldsen's studio in Rome. This experience had left him, against the general tendency of mid-Victorian taste, with an inclination, not for Gothic, but for Renaissance principles. His early work at Somerset House, and for Hoole and Company at Sheffield, reflects this inspiration. He breathed a heavily charged Renaissance vitality into the commercial metalwork of the company exhibited at the 1851 exhibition. These activities gave rise to his recognition by a group of followers—Hugh Stannus, Godfrey Sykes, James Gamble and Reuben Townroe, whose work in the Victoria and Albert Museum Refreshment Room and elsewhere in the 1860s was a collaborative venture of great interest. Reuben Townroe's design for a stained glass window, illustrated in Fig. 77, shows the good results that could be obtained by the old, academic teaching tradition.

Another designer who spent two years as a pupil at Somerset House from the age of 13 to 15 was Christopher Dresser (1834–1904), although

77 Reuben Townroe, *They builded them houses*, design for a stained glass window in the Victoria and Albert Museum which was destroyed by enemy action in the Second World War (Victoria and Albert Museum)

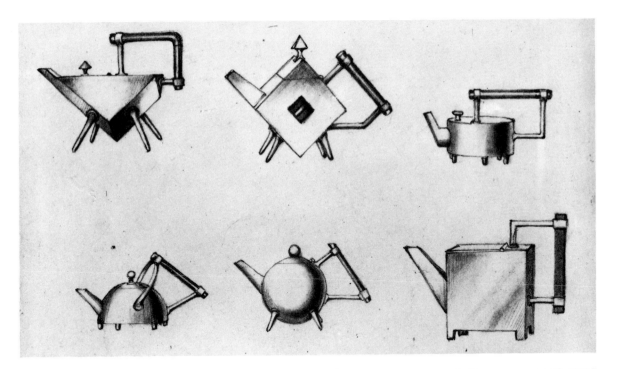

78 Designs for teapots from
The Art of Decorative Design
by Christopher Dresser
(Victoria and Albert Museum)

79 Silver kettle and stand,
attributed to Christopher
Dresser, hallmarked
Birmingham, 1895 (Fine Art
Society)

he was to benefit more from his later contact with a leading member of the Cole circle, Owen Jones. A Doctor of Botany, Dresser brought to his theories of design a systematically trained mind which finds written expression in his *Principles of Design* (1873), with its carefully worked out laws on the application of spouts and handles to pouring vessels, with results of startling cubistic modernity. Dresser's work, like that of the poet Gerard Manley Hopkins, has been more influential on the twentieth century than it was during his own lifetime. Like Hopkins, he had a more mystical side, admiring 'the power, energy, force or vigour' that he saw in 'the bursting buds of Spring', and this appreciation of plant forms can be seen in the water lily leaf structure of the sweet-meat bowl (Fig. 80), which also reflects his words, 'curves will be found to be more beautiful as they are subtle in character'. His remarkable versatility of taste is also shown in his appreciation of Egyptian and Pre-Columbian art—the Egyptian influence appearing in the tripod feet of the claret jug (Fig. 81).

To realize the full imaginative power of Dresser's work it is necessary to set it against the prosaic achievements brought about by the teachings of the National Art Training Schools. They had been established at South Kensington in 1852, and later through the country, by Sir Henry Cole, in order to improve design standards in manufacture, but achieved only one striking success of permanent importance in the history of the decorative arts. This was the result of the unique collaboration between the dynamic headmaster of the Lambeth School of Art, J. C. Sparkes, and Sir Henry Doulton (1820–1897).

The success of Doulton's vast pottery empire had been firmly laid by the 1860s in the innovatory field of sanitary fittings, sewer pipes, stoneware sinks and street gullies, a demand for these products having been created by the awakening Victorian awareness of the importance of hygiene. But these productions, although financially lucrative, and of great social value, could not fully realize Henry Doulton's ceramic ambitions. Highly intellectual, he was a keen reader of Wordsworth, whom he had met, and Ruskin, whose 'religion and beauty' and emphasis on instruction appealed to him, although the associated economic theories proved less acceptable.

Doulton served on the committee of the Lambeth School of Art, and Sparkes persuaded him to take a number of students into the works to assist in the ornamentation of professionally thrown stoneware pots, which he had begun to produce experimentally for the 1862 exhibition. From small beginnings at the Paris Exhibition of 1867 these productions became more ambitious and sought after, particularly the bold *sgraffito* decorations of Hannah Barlow, one of the most gifted of the new Doulton team, whose great speciality was the drawing of animals etched into the slip surface with a few rapidly drawn lines. Hannah's sister, Florence, specialized in a form of cameo-like *pâte sur pâte* in which depictions of birds were built up in low relief in coloured clays. Their brother Arthur Barlow, Eliza Simmance and Mark V. Marshall

80 Sweet-meat bowl in silver,
the interior gilded, designed
by Christopher Dresser,
1881–1882 (Fine Art Society)

81 Christopher Dresser, claret
jug in glass, with electro-
plated mounts, 1879,
manufactured by Huskin and
Heath (Fine Art Society)

82

83

82 Pottery, probably
Doultons, with women at
work ornamenting pots, artist
unknown (Victoria and Albert
Museum)

83 Hannah Barlow, saltglazed
Doulton vases (A. Gee, Esq)

84 Mark V. Marshall, Doulton
vase (R. Dennis, Esq)

all produced work of great originality for the firm. But the most gifted
artist was George Tinworth (1843–1913), whose strangely varied talents
were to lead him to produce both whimsical groups of humanized mice
and pixies, and terracotta reliefs which tell the Bible stories from the
Plymouth Brethren viewpoint with a strangely moving intensity.

These were only the best known names in the Doulton company's
output of art pottery. By the late 1870s, when the firm's production had
become well known and keenly collected, no less than three hundred
female artists were employed, all encouraged to express their individuality by signing their work with their monogram. It is this respect
for the individuality of the workman which makes the Doulton
contribution so remarkable in the commercial sphere, producing, in
spite of the division of labour, appreciative remarks from Ruskin, who
on a visit to the factory chose a Hannah Barlow because of 'the piggies
running round the rim'.

Although they were only briefly connected with the Doulton firm, it is
appropriate to mention here the work of the important precursors of the
studio pottery movement, the Martin Brothers, who, after early work
under Sparkes and at Doultons, established themselves at Southall,
Middlesex. There, between 1877 and 1915, they formed a unique working
unit, small and compact as only a family firm can be, yet remarkably
varied in the work they produced. Their best known productions were
their 'grotesques', the birds and other creatures so aptly described by

85

86

85 George Tinworth, Doulton
saltglaze groups showing
Punch and Judy and
Steeplechase (R. Dennis, Esq)

86 George Tinworth,
terracotta group, *The Woman
Touching Christ's Garment*
(R. Dennis Esq)

Cosmo Monkhouse: '. . . we have a hundred young sculptors who will model you a Venus or Adonis as soon as look at you; but who save Mr. Martin could give you a Boojum or Snark in the round'. But it would be wrong to give the impression that their work was only whimsical. After their visit to the Paris Exhibition of 1900 they began to produce pots inspired by the forms of melons, gourds and marrows, and developed a brilliant new range of surface textures which often imitated the skins of fish or lizards, works which have a freedom that gives the Martin Brothers their unique status as the first true Studio potters.

On the whole, however, by the 1880s, the National Art School system, dominated by an emphasis on fine art training, had become a most impractical one. Lethaby was to declare that the curriculum of the average art school made him think of learning to swim in a thousand lessons without water. Some of the blame for this state of affairs can be attributed to Edward Poynter (Director from 1875 to 1881), who was more interested in fine arts than design.

87 Martin Brothers, Southall, two small vases with incised decoration of fishes, 1896 (Victoria and Albert Museum)

88 R. W. Martin modelling a 'Martin' bird (Southall Public Library)

Thomas Armstrong, Poynter's successor, made a conscientious attempt to redress the balance, no doubt influenced by a report published in 1884 by a Royal Commission on Technical Instruction which stated: 'Industrial design has not received sufficient attention in art schools and classes ... there has been a great departure in this respect from the intention with which the schools of art were originally founded, viz, the practical application of knowledge of ornamental art to the improvement of manufactures'.

One Arts and Crafts figure, both practical and visionary, John Sedding, converted these oft reiterated aims into a battle cry. Listen to his words at the Liverpool Congress of 1888:

Fancy what a year of grace it were for England, if our industries were placed under the guidance of 'one vast Morris'. Fancy a Morris installed in every factory—the Joseph of every grinding Pharaoh. The battle of the industries were half won.

As a step towards this desirable state of affairs, Armstrong began to appoint as heads of Colleges of Art in manufacturing towns men who were in sympathy, not only with the fine arts, but also with the decorative arts which played a vital role in local industries. One such appointment was made in Birmingham, the centre of the jewellery trade.

The city of Birmingham throughout the nineteenth century enjoyed an unenviable reputation for the production of cheap and shoddy brass ornaments and gimcrack jewellery, imitative pieces which made 'Brummagem ware' a byword for the meretricious and third rate. Such productions were once memorably satirized in a cartoon by George Belcher in *Punch*. It depicts two visitors at a country sale. One is excitedly holding up a pot—saying, 'The auctioneer *said* it was Ming'. 'Yes', rejoins his friend, 'made by the man who put the "ming" in Birmingham'.

Victorian Birmingham was in reality a proud city, ruled by earnest, non-conformist dynastic families, who collected paintings of the Pre-Raphaelite School, and believed that the promotion of art education could aid the city's industries. The Birmingham School of Design, founded in 1843, had close associations with the nearby jewellery quarter. In 1888, on its move to new premises in Margaret Street, Morris and Burne-Jones both made highly successful visits to the new school, and their influence was paramount there. In the 1890s its dynamic new headmaster, Edward R. Taylor, whose son in the 1900s was to found the Ruskin Pottery, brought the teachings of Ruskin and Morris to bear on the staff and pupils of the school. He believed students should acquire a number of skills in media other than drawing and painting, and master various craft techniques, ideas which he published in a book, *Elementary Art Teaching*, in 1890.

A distinguished teacher at the school was Joseph Southall (1861–1944) who played a leading part in the revival of *tempera* painting, an activity with close links with Arts and Crafts theories. During the 1890s a partisan group of artists devoted to the tempera medium emerged at Birmingham. Most of the members of the group were pupils at the School of Art, many of them staying on to teach, among them Charles Gere (1869–1957) and Arthur Joseph Gaskin (1862–1928). Both men started their careers by working for the Kelmscott Press, Gere drawing the frontispiece for William Morris's *News from Nowhere*, and Gaskin producing illustrations for *The Shepherd's Calendar* in 1897. Gere later became well known for his work in *tempera, gesso* and gilding, but also continued to design in other fields, producing some striking embroidery. Gaskin, after illustrating some fairy stories, turned in 1899 to the design of jewellery, together with his wife, Georgina (1868–1934). Their work has an elaborate filigree quality, achieved by their skilful use of silver wire in scroll form, enhanced by their choice of stones: pale, cabochon-cut amethysts and mother-of-pearl, set in and surrounded by natural forms carried out in silver gilt and gold.

In 1890 Birmingham City Council established at Victoria Street a branch school specifically for jewellers' and silversmiths' apprentices, under the direction of Robert Catterson-Smith, a fine silversmith and draughtsman who had worked directly with Morris. In 1902, Gaskin succeeded Catterson-Smith as principal of the School, and was joined by John Paul Cooper as head of the metalwork department in 1904. Cooper,

89 Charles Gere's frontispiece to William Morris's *News from Nowhere*, Kelmscott Press, 1892

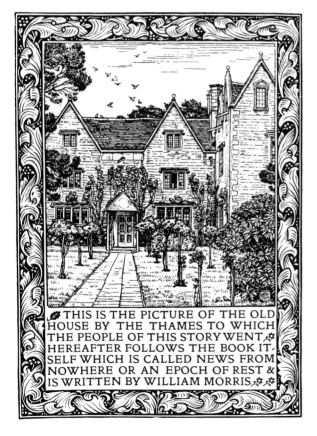

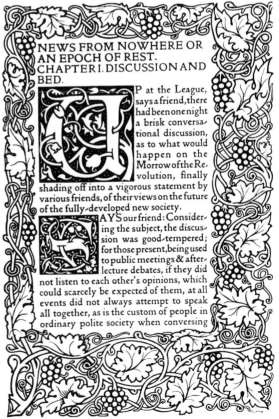

90 Charles Gere, banner embroidered in silk and metal thread on canvas, St. Mary the Virgin, Primrose Hill, London

91 John Paul Cooper, octagonal casket in walnut covered with modelled and gilded gessowork, 1902 (Fine Art Society)

92 John Paul Cooper, seated cupid pendant in silver set with a chrysoprase and two garnets, 1911 (Fine Art Society)

who had taken up metalwork on the advice of Henry Wilson in 1897, and at first worked for him, taught at Birmingham for three years. But the majority of his output, which ranks as some of the most remarkable Arts and Crafts metalwork, was produced later at a house he designed for himself at Westerham in Kent.

It is fascinating to trace the increasing sophistication of his forms. The engaging clumsiness of the *gesso* work on his early octagonal casket of 1902 gives place to the stylized pendant and Christening mug of the early 1920s. But perhaps the most elegant of all his productions are the boxes from the end of his career, covered in shagreen, a material in whose use he specialized.

The productions of these inspired teachers, and their pupils, such as Bernard Cuzner and Omar Ramsden, provided some of the most attractive exhibits in successive Arts and Crafts exhibitions, notably in that of 1903 in which their jewellery was shown to particular advantage. This concentration of talent also led inevitably to the foundation, in 1895, of a Guild. The Birmingham Guild of Handicraft's leading figure was Arthur Dixon (1856–1929) an architect whose best building was a Cathedral in Seoul, Korea, and who himself designed the Guild's own premises in Great Charles Street, a building which still survives the modern rape of the city centre and summarizes admirably Arts and Crafts principles, epitomized in the Guild's motto, 'By Hammer and Hand'. Dixon himself, however, was, like Benson, not wholly opposed to the use of the machine. A catalogue produced for the Ideal Home Exhibition at Olympia in 1910 states; 'In the purely ornamental part of the Guild's work, machinery plays no part: but in the constructional parts the most perfect and scientific accuracy is guaranteed'. Guild

93 John Paul Cooper, silver
christening mug, 1911 (Fine
Art Society)

94 John Paul Cooper,
octagonal box covered in
shagreen, mounted in silver
(Fine Art Society)

95 John Paul Cooper, walnut
box covered in rough natural
shagreen, mounted in silver
with a knob in the form of a
cormorant, 1920 (Fine Art
Society)

96 Bernard Cuzner, bowl in silver, with embossed, chased and applied foliage decoration, set with mother of pearl and semi-precious stones, inscribed *Labore et Virtute*, Birmingham hallmark, 1905–6 (the Warwickshire Justices)

pieces were in fact simple in shape, executed in base metals, with decoration limited to hammered surfaces, softly rather than brilliantly polished. In this practice, as in his holding the ideal of the cooperative nature of the Guild, Dixon was influenced by the example of his friend C. R. Ashbee, while from his close association with William Morris arose his concern with the division of labour: 'a man should not be cut off from the full effect of his work . . . if art is to live and not die, men's work must be so arranged that they may be able to keep their souls alive . . . the craftsmen must come before the merchant, and the machine must be subservient to the hand of man'. Dixon and the Guild put such exhortations into practice, more effectively than more idealistic ventures, by aiming deliberately at the involvement and membership of manufacturing craftsmen. As a result, entirely commercial Birmingham firms* were greatly influenced by their style.

It would however be wrong to give the impression that Dixon's crusade against the 'public demand for knick knacks and drawing room ornaments' fostered by businessmen who cater for a 'world . . . in need of so many millions of candlesticks every year', was completely successful. Nowhere in fact more than Birmingham, were the 'insidious tendrils' of the Art Nouveau style to cling tighter to the 'sturdy plant' of Arts and Crafts ideology. For Birmingham was one of the great centres for Art

*That of A. E. Jones, for example.

87

97 Arthur S. Dixon, hammered silver coffee pot with finial and handle of fruitwood, Birmingham Guild of Handicraft, Birmingham hallmark, 1901 (Fine Art Society)

98 Pewter cake tray, probably designed by Archibald Knox, *c.* 1904, made by the firm of W. H. Haseler for Liberty & Company (Victoria and Albert Museum)

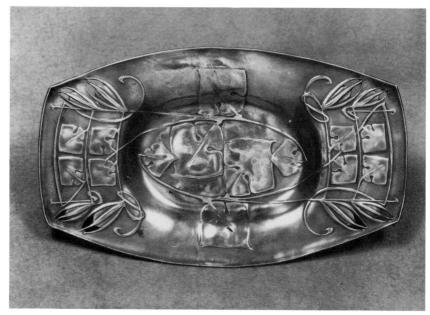

99 Copper jar and cover and brass kettle by Arthur S. Dixon, c. 1895–1900 (Victoria and Albert Museum)

Nouveau metalwork productions, the home of 'Cymric' and 'Tudric' silver and pewter work produced by the firm of W. H. Haseler for Liberty and Company, a name synonymous with the new style. Indeed Archibald Knox, their principal silver designer, had been dismissed from his art teaching post at Kingston for corrupting his students' taste by introducing them to Art Nouveau designs. Haseler's productions for Liberty's aroused the ire of C. R. Ashbee, who felt that his own work was both plagiarized and degraded by the manufacturer, whom he described satirically as 'Mr. Novelty'. Ashbee particularly disliked such deviations from the 'strict gospel' of Arts and Crafts ideology as the practice of adding 'hand wrought' distressing onto the surface of a machine-finished piece. Today when such polemics amuse rather than shock, one can only agree with the compilers of the admirable catalogue of *Birmingham Gold and Silver Work 1773–1973*, who selected a Knox piece as the frontispiece to the volume as being one of the finest productions of the city's varied work in this field.

100 Archibald Knox, teapot in
pewter made by the firm of
W. Haseler for Liberty and
Company, stamped 'Tudric
Pewter', 1903 (Victoria and
Albert Museum)

101 Archibald Knox, hot
water jug, also part of the
Tudric range (Victoria and
Albert Museum)

If Birmingham's flowering as a centre for Arts and Crafts metalwork owes much of its original inspiration to the gifted teacher E. H. Taylor, Glasgow's debt to the director of its College of Art during this period is even more profound, for his work established the city as an internationally known centre of advanced design. F. H. Newbery (1855–1946) was himself a trained product of the centralized system of art education at South Kensington and was appointed by Armstrong as head of the Glasgow College in 1885. Although himself a painter of great ability, he showed from the start of his appointment an active interest in fostering craft teaching. In this he was perhaps encouraged by an open letter to Glasgow art students written by Walter Crane in 1887, which described the aspirations of would be designers thus:

There is room for the highest qualities in the pattern of a carpet, the design of a wallpaper, a bit of *repoussée* or wrought iron or wood carving. The sincere designer and craftsman ... with his invention and skill applied to the accessories of everyday life may do more to keep alive the sense of beauty than the greatest painter that ever lived.

Newbery himself, at a lecture delivered at the Edinburgh congress of the National Association for the Advancement of Art and its Application to

102 An ink-stand in pewter, part of the Tudric range for Liberty and Company (Victoria and Albert Museum)

103 Sir George Frampton, rosewater dish bearing a London hallmark, 1903–4 (the Merchant Taylor's Company)

103

Industry in 1889, amplified and reinforced these views: 'Picture painting is for the few; beauty in the common surroundings of our daily lives is, or should be, an absolute necessity to the many.' And, in reply to a question, he stated that seventy-five per cent of his students applied their teaching to handicraft, and only twenty-five per cent to the painting of pictures. In the following year, 1890, Newbery invited Lewis F. Day to lecture to the school on 'Art and Handicraft', and such lectures became a regular feature of the School's activities. Significantly, when Charles Rennie Mackintosh (1868–1928), the brilliant young architect and part-time student of the school, looked in 1892 for a motto for Glasgow designers he selected an aphorism by J. D. Sedding, the leading English Arts and Crafts designer: 'There is hope in honest error: none in the icy perfections of the mere stylist'.

As a result of this stimulus, and a series of lectures on Arts and Crafts in the autumn of 1893, a group of students held in 1894 an exhibition of furniture, metalwork and embroidery of a completely original character. The group comprized the architects Mackintosh and Herbert MacNair (1868–1955), and the sisters Margaret (1865–1933) and Frances (1874–1921) Macdonald. The origins of the style of the 'Glasgow Four' are more complex than is generally realized. The nickname, the 'spook' school, which was promptly attached to their work, was derived from their admiration for the drawings of Jan Toorop and Aubrey Beardsley, which they had seen reproduced in the first issues of *The Studio* magazine. But equally important as an inspirational source for their designs was the work of Christopher Dresser, E. W. Godwin, Walter Crane, A. H. Mackmurdo and C. F. A. Voysey, which they also absorbed through such periodicals as the *Hobby Horse, The Builder* and the *Magazine of Art*.

104 Motto designed by C. R. Mackintosh

Mackintosh was able to see actual examples of the work of Voysey, the only source he personally acknowledged for the design of his furniture, at the fifth Arts and Crafts exhibition, held in 1896, at which the Glasgow group exhibited some twenty pieces. Unfortunately their work was unfavourably received, its functional elements being ignored and hostile criticism being directed at what were regarded as its dangerous tendencies towards the fraught tangles of continental Art Nouveau. The Group was never again invited to exhibit at an Arts and Crafts Society show, and relations between Walter Crane and Francis Newbery became positively chilly after Newbery's attack in the September, 1902, issue of *The Studio* on the English Arts and Crafts Society's exhibition in Turin.

This estrangement illustrates particularly clearly the complexity of the dichotomy between Art Nouveau and Arts and Crafts principles. Why were the Glasgow Group's productions so frowned on by English designers? The question today is hard to answer, for a visit to the library of Mackintosh's inspired building, the Glasgow College of Art, reveals individual chairs, tables, electric light fittings which all speak of the individuality of the craftsman and repudiation of machine mass

106

105 Sir George Frampton,
'Peter Pan'. Bronze reduction
of the statue in Kensington
Gardens (Fine Art Society)

106 R. Anning Bell's *Mother
and Child*, plaster relief,
coloured and gilt, 1896 (Fine
Art Society)

107 F. Cayley Robinson's
illustration to Materlinck's
Blue Bird (Victoria and
Albert Museum)

107

production which were such a feature of Arts and Crafts ideology. Yet the room, although Arts and Crafts in individual detail, is far more forward-looking than any other building by an architect of the movement, being indeed one of the first great modern interiors.

If the Glasgow School's relationship with the Arts and Crafts movement was an unhappy one, the establishment in 1896 of the Central School for Arts and Crafts in Holborn must be accounted one of its greatest triumphs. That it was and remains so important an educational institution is almost wholly attributable to its principal founder, William Richard Lethaby. He was born at Barnstaple in Devon, the son of a carver and picture framer. Education at the local grammar school and school of art led to him being articled to a local architect. His work soon brought academic recognition, and after a short period in Derbyshire he was invited to join Norman Shaw's office in 1879 where he remained until 1890, acting as Chief Assistant. His active role in the Kenton and Company furniture enterprise and his friendship with William Morris made him an eminently suitable candidate when in 1894 he applied for the post of Inspector of Art Schools for the L.C.C. In his reference for Lethaby, Morris wrote, 'I have found him a man of great enthusiasm for the best side of art and much power into seeing into the essentials of art, without being too much bothered by conventional views of the subject matter: he is a keen and minute critic of detail and has a good knowledge of and sympathy for the practical and experimental side of the crafts.' Success in his new post led in 1896 to Lethaby's being appointed as joint principal with the sculptor George Frampton of the Central School of Arts and Crafts. In practice Lethaby took complete charge, for Frampton's work as sculptor (he was creator of the statue of Peter Pan in Kensington Gardens) left him little time for administration.

It was above all Lethaby's inspired gift for detecting emergent talents and engaging them as instructors, that made the school during his directorship a teaching institution unequalled in Europe. Lethaby was of course not alone in hiring artists and craftsmen on a part-time basis. Newbery in Glasgow employed such figures as R. Anning Bell (1863–1933) and F. Cayley Robinson (1862–1927) but they were already established artists who had made their reputations elsewhere. What made Lethaby's achievements so unique was his ability to spot the truly original qualities of individual creators, and like Diaghilev with the Ballet Russe, weld into a galaxy of talent people who would have 'hesitated at anyone else's request to sacrifice their time to teaching.'

By far the most remarkable of all Lethaby's finds was Edward Johnston (1872–1944). At their first meeting, Lethaby was so impressed by the unknown young man's work, that he commissioned and paid for a manuscript, and remarked that he was thinking of starting an illuminating class at the Central School the following winter. 'If all's well', said Lethaby, 'I shall put you in charge of it'. The first class started in 1899, with many pupils, ranging from the sixty year old Cobden

Addendum: A Fifteenth Century Carol (from "A.E.Carols", ed. by E.Rickert, 1910.): Invented with too soft a Reed & Mended by E.J. 11th Dr. 1935. Ad which is wrong.& so this MS is "spoilt".

This MS was written in a hurry for a Village Show, & it being thereby spoilt, I determined to present it to Mr. Sidney Cockerell, one of my most valued guides who (tho' he never spoilt me) is able to appreciate good intentions. E.J. 23.xij. 35.

Adam lay ybounden,
Bounden in a bond;
Four thousand winter
Thought he not too long.
And all was for an apple,
An apple that he took,
As clerkës finden written
  In their book.
Nor had the apple taken been,
The apple taken been,
Then had never our Lady
A-been heaven's queen.
Blessed be the time
That apple taken was!
Therefore we may singen
  Deo gracias!

109

109 Edward Johnston's 'Adam lay ybounden'. Only a perfectionist of genius like Johnston could describe this *tour de force* as spoilt (Victoria and Albert Museum)

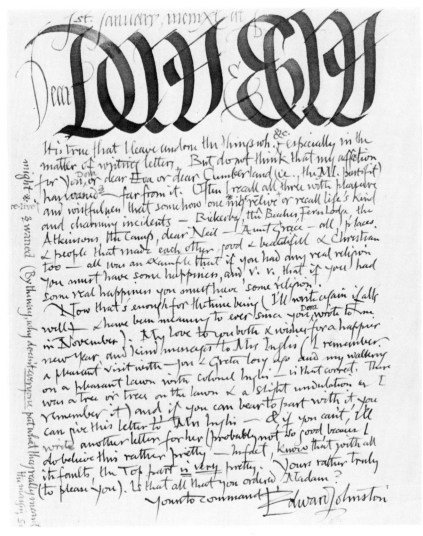

110 Edward Johnston, a personal letter to friends. As he writes, 'with all its faults, the top part *is very* pretty' (the Craft Study Centre, Bath)

Sanderson to others who were to become famous, notably the young Eric Gill, whose 'Gill Sans' typeface has so changed the face of modern printing.

Johnston may indeed justly claim to be the Arts and Crafts figure whose work has most influenced the public. His classic work *Writing and Illuminating and Lettering*, 1906, probably the finest text book ever written on a practical subject, is still in print and in use. Every day the entire population of London benefits from the clarity and legibility of his typeface, designed 'with the austerity of an engineer', for London Transport in 1916, on the initiative of its inspired Traffic Development Officer, and great patron of the Arts, Frank Pick (1878–1941). His utter integrity as a calligrapher can be seen in all his widely divergent works. His daughter, Priscilla, in her delightful biography of her father, has told of his difficulties in answering mundane letters, arising from his feelings that every work of his pen must be a work of art, as the personal letter illustrated (Fig. 110) so amusingly shows.

Other distinguished teachers at the Central School in its early years included Douglas Cockerell, himself a pupil of Cobden-Sanderson, who taught bookbinding; J. H. Mason, chief compositor of the Doves Press, who taught printing; Alexander Fisher, who taught enamelling; George Jack of the Morris Firm, who taught furniture design; Halsey Ricardo, who taught architecture—a roll of honour of remarkable brilliance.

One more teacher at the school must be singled out for special mention—Henry Wilson, who taught metalwork there from 1896. Wilson, whose textbook, *Silverwork and Metalwork*, 1903, remains a standard working manual, had a complex personality. Both his architecture and his metalwork are distinguished by his remarkable use of symbolism, a reflection of his widely diverse literary and religious interests. He first began to practice metalwork in 1890, and in 1895 set up

111 Crozier by Henry Wilson
(from an original photograph)
(Victoria and Albert Museum)

112 Henry Wilson, pendant
cross (left) set with a baroque
pearl (Mrs Laurence Hodson);
necklace and pendant (right)
in the form of a peacock
(Mrs F. Gibson)

113 Alexander Fisher,
overmantle in bronze, ivory,
enamels and semi-precious
stones, 1900 (Fine Art Society)

114 Wallpaper designed by Henry Wilson in 1896 for Jeffrey & Co (Victoria and Albert Museum)

115 Chalice by Henry Wilson in silver, partly gilt, with cast, chased and applied ornament and repoussé knob in the form of a grotesque monster enamelled in blue and green, mounted in carved ivory, for St. Bartholomew's, Brighton, 1898

114

115

his own metalworking shop, a few years later entering into a brief partnership with Alexander Fisher. Wilson's dramatic architectural and metalwork style are both seen to their finest advantage in St. Bartholomew's Church, Brighton, 1897–1908, both building and plate possessing affinities with the imaginary productions of his friend the theatrical genius Gordon Craig (1872–1966), who dreamt of a national theatre designed by Wilson. Equally remarkable, but less known, is St. Mark's Church, Brithdir, Merionethshire, 1895–1897. In 1905 he designed the bronze doors for the Anglican Cathedral of St. John the Divine, New York.

Such were the achievements of three of the most remarkable Schools of Art of those years. The influences of the traditions they established are still felt today.

6

Houses for Art Lovers: the Widening Vision

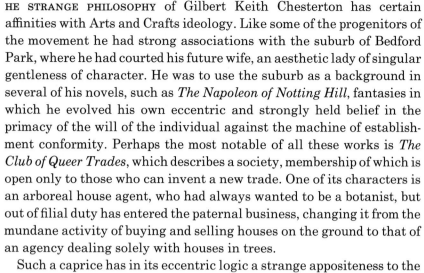

HE STRANGE PHILOSOPHY of Gilbert Keith Chesterton has certain affinities with Arts and Crafts ideology. Like some of the progenitors of the movement he had strong associations with the suburb of Bedford Park, where he had courted his future wife, an aesthetic lady of singular gentleness of character. He was to use the suburb as a background in several of his novels, such as *The Napoleon of Notting Hill*, fantasies in which he evolved his own eccentric and strongly held belief in the primacy of the will of the individual against the machine of establishment conformity. Perhaps the most notable of all these works is *The Club of Queer Trades*, which describes a society, membership of which is open only to those who can invent a new trade. One of its characters is an arboreal house agent, who had always wanted to be a botanist, but out of filial duty has entered the paternal business, changing it from the mundane activity of buying and selling houses on the ground to that of an agency dealing solely with houses in trees.

Such a caprice has in its eccentric logic a strange appositeness to the architectural fantasies of one of the most distinguished Arts and Crafts architects, Mackay Hugh Baillie Scott (1865–1945). On his tombstone, a simple cubic stele at Edenbridge in Kent, is carved the inscription, 'Nature he loved, and next to Nature, Art'. Few architects of his time came closer to expressing in the design of his small houses, with their hob-goblin cosyness, the strengths and weaknesses implicit in such a credo. Like the character in Chesterton's novel, Baillie Scott actually built in 1898 a house in a tree, aptly named 'Le Nid', a royal log cabin, supported by a group of eight living trees, built in a forest in Romania for the twenty-three year old Crown Princess Marie. Her description of the building has the true Rapunzel ring of fairy tale:

116 Interior of *Le Nid*, Sinaia, Romania, M. H. Baillie Scott, *Houses and Gardens*, 1906

My imagination was full of tales. I was not growing fast enough and my dreams were haunting me, so that I thought of a house among the tree tops . . . a plain hut, made of tree trunks, hung among a few fir trees. You could only reach it by climbing the steep staircase of a wooden tower, from which a drawbridge was lowered. Once you reached the other side, the bridge was lifted and my house was like an inconquerable citadel.

How did a commission for a citadel for a beautiful young princess in Romania come to be given to a romantic young architect in the Isle of Man? And how does the sober earnestness, and parochial introversion of the English Arts and Crafts movement suddenly come to be known so far afield? To find the answer we must turn to consider the wide-spread dissemination of one of the most influential of all art periodicals, *The Studio* magazine, founded in 1893. When we look in a library today at the serried rows of green volumes of the magazine from its foundation to the present day,* it is hard to imagine the initial impact that this publication had on the artistic concerns of its formative years. From its first number, which contained an article by Aylmer Vallance that

*At the time of writing, *Studio International* has just tragically finally foundered.

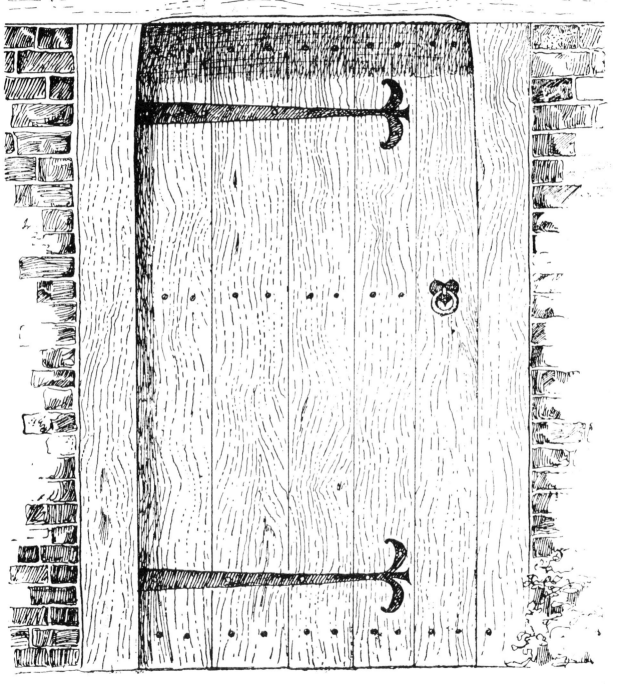

117 Design for a front door by
M. H. Baillie Scott, *The
Studio*, April, 1895

virtually made the reputation of Aubrey Beardsley, the magazine became and remained of paramount importance as an artistic force. There had, of course, been art periodicals before, notably the Cole oriented *Art Journal*, and of course the *Hobby Horse*, but none so consistently concerned with the emergence of new ideas. This made it an ideal platform for the promulgation of both Art Nouveau style, and Arts and Crafts ideology, both in well illustrated articles and in its keenly contested monthly competitions. Its rapid international success can be gauged by its impact on such different readers as the young Picasso in Barcelona, and Diaghilev in St. Petersburg. His magazine *Mir Ikkuskva* (The World of Art) 1800, the Austrian *Ver Sacrum*, 1898, the German *Pan*, 1895 and *Dekorative Kunst*, 1897 and a host of other publications in Europe and America were founded more or less in emulation of *The Studio*'s example. Together they formed an incestuous, cross-pollinating international art press, all keenly aware of the editorial policies and articles of their rivals. The appearance of an article on, or by, a new English artist, craftsman, or architect could, as never before, lead to a rapid national and, ironically, even more international fame. A striking example of this process can be cited. Gleeson White's appreciative article of 1898 on the Glasgow Four in *The Studio* started a rapidly developing appreciation of their work. This led to their wild acclaim in Vienna in 1900, when cheering students removed the horses from C. R. Mackintosh's carriage to drag it triumphantly through the streets, a response which was in striking contrast to the indifference with which his work was greeted at home.

In no field was this international recognition more appreciative of British innovatory ideas than in that of architecture, particularly of small 'artistic' houses. Ever since, in 1859, Philip Webb had designed the 'Red House' for William Morris, and Norman Shaw in the 1870s had created his 'aesthetic elysium' at Bedford Park, a continuing concern had developed among young architects for the problems involved in designing small houses. This concern evolved naturally from Morris's concern for the home and its furnishings as a complete expression of individual artistic taste, an urge to gain complete control of at least the environment one lived in, even if wider Utopian visions of ideal communities proved impractical. Architecture, and the crafts thus found their perfect expression in the design of the house, and these dual concerns are reflected in the careers of Mackmurdo, Lethaby, Gimson, and Ashbee, who all followed the example of Morris himself, in studying architecture and then turning to the crafts.

An idea derived from these concerns which was later to be greatly developed, found its first expression in a design by Mackmurdo, published in *The British Architect* in 1889, a 'House for an Artist'. Houses for artists, designed by artists, were to become a regular feature of architectural competitions in the next twenty years. In this, the first of such designs, all our attention is directed to the exterior features of the building. A classical pediment is flanked by the shallow slender

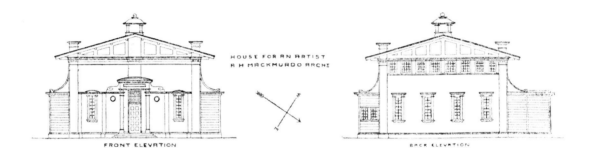

118 House for an Artist,
c. 1887, A. H. Mackmurdo.
Originally published in *The
British Architect*, January 4th,
1889 and later reproduced in
The *Hobby Horse*

pilasters, and flat-topped finials, the unmistakable thumbprint of Mackmurdo's decorative style. Such finials were to be adopted by C. F. A. Voysey (1857–1941), one of the most systematic exponents of both the architectural and craft principles of the movement.

Voysey's career as an architect began relatively slowly after he set up in practice in 1882. To keep himself occupied, on the advice of Mackmurdo, he began to design wallpapers and textiles, which were boldly stylized in a manner that led him to be regarded as a precursor of Art Nouveau style. He was later to repudiate this belief vigorously, for he personally found Art Nouveau 'distinctly unhealthy and revolting'. His own views can be learnt from an interview in *The Studio* in 1893, which first brought him widespread recognition, and illustrated his metalwork, wallpapers and furniture. In it he said, 'Let us begin by discarding the mass of useless ornaments and banishing the millinery that degrades our furniture and fittings. Reduce the variety of patterns and colours in a room. Eschew all imitations and have each thing the best of its sort'. Much of the appeal in Voysey's designs derives from his adherence to these principles, his avoidance of all fussiness, and the stark simplicity of his linear patterns. This simplicity is seen to particularly powerful effect in the bold silhouettes of his metalwork. He also designed some vigorous alphabets.

Above: 'The Summoning of the Knights', a Merton
Abbey tapestry for the Holy Grail series at Stanmore
Hall designed by William Morris and Edward Burne-
Jones (Munich, Münchner Stadtmuseum)

Right: Firescreen, 1884, designed by A. H.
Mackmurdo and executed by the Century Guild
(William Morris Gallery, photo: Clive Friend)

Opposite: Peacock pendant, silver set with pearls, 1900, designed by C. R. Ashbee and executed by the Guild and School of Handicrafts (Victoria and Albert Museum)

Above: Biscuit box, pewter set with blue-green enamels, 1903–4, designed by Archibald Knox and made by W. H. Haseler for Liberty and Company (Victoria and Albert Museum)

Top right: Pendant in the form of a sailing boat, enamelled gold set with an opal and hung with three amethysts, c. 1903, and peacock of gold enamelled and set with chrysoprases, 1903, designed by C. R. Ashbee and made by the Guild and School of Handicrafts (Victoria and Albert Museum)

Right: Necklace of silver set with opals and tourmalines and paste, c. 1914, designed and made by Arthur Gaskin (Victoria and Albert Museum)

Right: The bed recess in the master bedroom, Hill House, Helensburgh, 1908, architect Charles Rennie Mackintosh (Royal Incorporation of Architects in Scotland)

Below: C. R. Mackintosh's design for a 'House for an Art Connoisseur', his competition entry at the exhibition held in Darmstadt in 1901, 'A Document of German Art'

Opposite, top: Project for a hall by Will Bradley originally published as part of a series in the *Ladies' Home Journal* 1901–5 (reproduced from *Documents d'Architecture Moderne*)

Opposite, bottom: M. H. Baillie Scott's competition entry for the 'House for an Art Connoisseur' competition at the Darmstadt exhibition, 1901

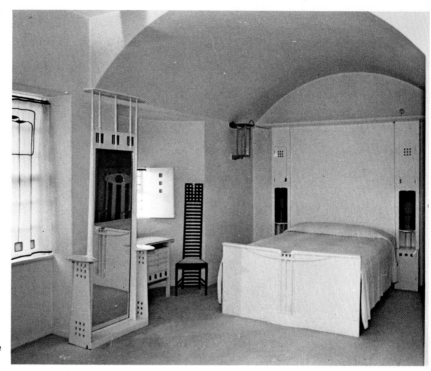

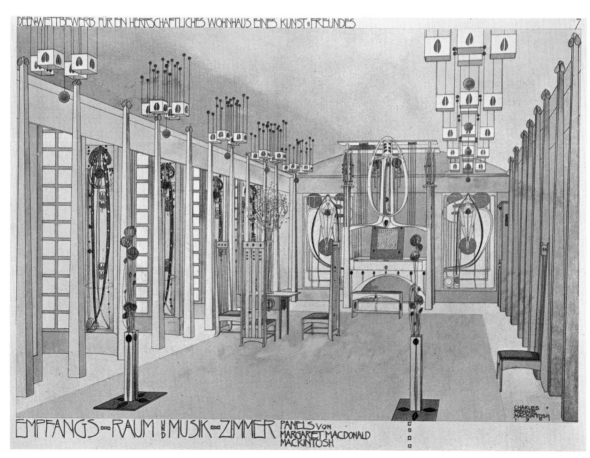

Above and right: Stucco and tile decorations used on the exteriors of two houses on the Matildenhöhe Art Colony, Darmstadt, 1899

Above and opposite: Two
views of Rodmarton Manor,
Gloucestershire, designed by
Ernest Barnsley, 1909–29

Right: Dresser, candlesticks
and box by Ernest Gimson
with pottery by Grace
Barnsley (Mrs F. L. M. Griggs)

Overleaf: Cabinet by Sidney
Barnsley with pottery
decorated by Grace Barnsley
(Mrs F. L. M. Griggs)

119 'Cereus' wallpaper by
C. F. A. Voysey (Victoria and
Albert Museum)

120 Silk and wool textile,
c. 1899, C. F. A. Voysey
(Victoria and Albert Museum)

121 Design for projecting
metalwork shop sign, 1902,
C. F. A Voysey (Victoria and
Albert Museum)

The same qualities are inherent in the structural forms of Voysey's buildings, as exemplified in a well known house of 1891 at Bedford Park which has striking white walls, and a gawky, yet exciting, sense of verticality. They became modified in his later houses, which have a traditional quality derived from the vernacular English seventeenth-century yeoman house, handled with an unostentatious yet powerful originality. His designs for the Norwich Union Insurance offices, one of his rare commercial projects, show how he could use these qualities in the dignified and austere setting of a board room.

Throughout his long career Voysey was to be one of the most regular of all exhibitors at the Arts and Crafts Exhibition Society's shows. His work is, indeed, the most complete expression of the Society's aims, for it brings together the building, furnishing and decoration of the house as a total art form.

122 Chair and writing desk in oak with brass hinges and fittings, C. F. A. Voysey, 1896 (Victoria and Albert Museum)

123 Coffee pot, teapot and muffin dish, *c.* 1900, C. F. A. Voysey (Victoria and Albert Museum)

124 'Peacock' wallpaper by C. F. A. Voysey (Victoria and Albert Museum)

122

123

125 Alphabets by C. F. A.
Voysey. from *A Book of
Alphabets*, E. Strange, 1906

AABCDDE
EFGHAIJK·
LLMMCCNº
OP2QRSST
UVWXYZ·
12345678?
9º FE·AND
ABCDEFGHI
JKLMNOPQ·

126 Design for Norwich
Union Insurance Office Board
Room, C. F. A. Voysey
(Victoria and Albert Museum)

Like Voysey, Baillie Scott first achieved widespread recognition for his work in the pages of *The Studio* magazine. His first contribution to the journal in December, 1894 was in the humble role of competitor in a typical *Studio* competition—an attempt to design the 'Ideal Coal Scuttle'! But in the next issue, January, 1895, he published the first of many articles which were to establish his reputation as an architectural theorist of great originality. The article was prosaically entitled, against his own wishes, 'An Ideal Suburban House'. Yet, with hindsight, the editor of *The Studio*, Gleeson White, cannot be too adversely criticized for this mundane choice of headline. Baillie Scott, like G. K. Chesterton, had a deeply romantic vision, the power of seeing the extraordinary in the ordinary, and of treating the most prosaic building project with imaginative originality. His ideas can best be described in his own words. In 1896 he fulminated in the columns of *The Studio*:

The usual method for designing a small house may thus be formulated: Take a comparatively large house with the full complement of rooms . . . and compress the plan till all the rooms are reduced to the smallest possible dimensions. Then augment these cramped conditions by filling these rooms with heavy furniture . . . The final results of this scheme . . . will probably be that the family . . . will inhabit, perhaps, only one of these [rooms] and keep the others damp and musty for a special occasion which never comes.

It was Baillie Scott's mission to change this restricted 'Pooteresque' situation by creating complex and imaginative spaces which united halls and reception rooms into striking new spatial relationships. In his book *A Small Country House* published in 1897, he was to develop these ideas further:

The natural reaction from the dry mechanical routine of modern life leads to a demand for Romance in every form. In the form of fiction it supplies a retreat, an escape for the mind to an enchanted realm where thrilling deeds may be done without danger, and beautiful habitations enjoyed without expense. In the treatment of the house a more real and permanent haven may be secured. Here at least we may say there should be no ugliness. On crossing the threshold we pass into charmed territory, where everything we possess shall be in harmony.

Baillie Scott's dream in this passage again reminds us of one of the new trades—an Adventure and Romance Agency—in Chesterton's *Club of Queer Trades*. With poetic appositeness this belief in Romance was to be rewarded, as in a fairy story, by the appearance of a Prince and Fairy Godmother combined. His articles and book brought him the opportunity to design, not the small house of his dreams, but a real Palace for the Grand Duke of Hesse at Darmstadt.

It is difficult to summarize in words the character and achievements of this ideal patron, Ernst Ludwig, Grand Duke of Hesse. A portrait by Franz Stuck does it far more cogently in visual terms, showing in his face and bearing that peculiar blend of sensitivity, ruthlessness, and deep appreciation of the arts which was to enable him to make

127

128

127, 128 Designs for the
Dining Room (top) and Sitting
Room at the Darmstadt Palace
by M. H. Baillie Scott,
Building News, 1897

129 Baillie Scott, child's
chair with inlaid decoration
made at the Pyghtle Works,
Bedford, *c.* 1901 (Sir Andrew
McTaggart)

130, 131 Decorated
cabinets with painted tulips,
lilies, pinks and birds
designed by Baillie Scott
(*The Studio*)

132 Embroideries designed by
Baillie Scott and executed by
Mrs. Scott in 1903 (Victoria
and Albert Museum)

Darmstadt as important a mecca for lovers of 'jugendstil' and the Arts and Crafts as Bayreuth is for admirers of Wagner. His appreciation of the English Arts and Crafts movement, which was to have such far-reaching results, may in part have been prompted by an article by Baillie Scott in *The Studio* in April, 1897. Entitled 'On the Choice of Simple Furniture' it advocated simplicty and integration in interior design 'without reference to conventional ideas or the dictates of fashion'. By July of the same year, Baillie Scott had been commissioned to re-decorate and furnish the dining and sitting rooms at the Darmstadt palace, a somewhat similar commission going at the same time to C. R. Ashbee. In the event a degree of collaboration seems to have been achieved, the designs being Baillie Scott's, but the furniture, metalwork and light fittings all being executed by the Guild and School of

132

M. H. Baillie Scott in 1904

133 'The Latest Style of Room Decoration. The Home Made Beautiful According to the "Arts and Crafts" ', *Punch*, March 11, 1903

Handicrafts. Baillie Scott's daring colour schemes in orange, white enamel and hand-embossed leather, and his use of brightly painted tulips and roses on the walls, while hardly revolutionary, attracted immense attention, surpassed only by the novelty of the furniture, which became the theme for numerous articles.

Punch, as always alert to the possibilities of satirizing a new decorative trend, published a particularly apt cartoon in 1903, specifically directed at Baillie Scott who himself sits nervously reading the paper below a stencilled frieze of Manx cats. Behind him stand a cabinet and a 'Manx' piano, both similar to examples in the Palace at Darmstadt. An actual example of a 'Manx Piano, his ingenious attempt to solve "the strange case of the Victorian Piano" ' a perennial design problem, is also illustrated for comparison. But perhaps the most interesting feature of the cartoon is the barrel chair in the foreground, also of a type designed for the palace. This chair has an intriguing ancestry. When Burne-Jones designed the Merton Abbey tapestry 'The Summoning of the Knights', he had constructed several barrel chairs after a well known mediaeval prototype. Baillie Scott, who probably saw the tapestries when they were exhibited at the 1893 Arts and Crafts show, utilized the same shape for his own purposes. Mackintosh also used the form for the chairs that accompanied the 'domino' table in his tea rooms.

THE LATEST STYLE OF ROOM DECORATION. THE HOME MADE BEAUTIFUL.
According to the " Arts and Crafts."

134 Portrait of Ernst Ludwig
in the Palace at Darmstadt,
1902 (Stadtarchiv, Darmstadt)

134

135 A Manx piano designed   135
by M. H. Baillie Scott
(Victoria and Albert Museum)

136 Detail from the piano
illustrated, M. H. Baillie Scott
(Victoria and Albert Museum)

137 Tapestry, 'The
Summoning of the Knights',
Morris and Burne-Jones
(Münchner Stadt Museum,
Munich)

138 'The Summoning of the
Knights' being woven at the
Merton Works (William
Morris Gallery)

138

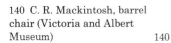

139 Barrel chair designed by Baillie Scott for the Darmstadt Palace (Victoria and Albert Museum)

140 C. R. Mackintosh, barrel chair (Victoria and Albert Museum)

140

Despite the humour of *Punch*, the Darmstadt commission, so widely publicized, had important consequences. Inspired by the success of the project, in 1899 Ernst Ludwig invited seven German and Austrian artists to form a colony in Darmstadt, and create their own houses on the hill, the Mathildenhöhe. Among those invited were Peter Behrens, who came from Munich, and Joseph Maria Olbrich, who came from Vienna, where in 1898 he had designed the building for the Vienna Secession.

The group's exhibition in 1901, 'A Document of German Art', was an artistic event of major significance, which would have been unthinkable without the initial catalyst of Baillie Scott and C. R. Ashbee's example. The colony's houses, grouped around the official buildings by Olbrich, the only professional architect in the group, marked the stylistic ascendancy of design principles evolved from the English Arts and Crafts movement, over the curvilinear Art Nouveau style which had reached its high point at the Paris exhibition of 1900. In the interior decoration of the buildings the debt to the English movement's productions was particularly clear.

117

141 Peter Behrens Haus, Darmstadt, part of the new artists' colony created under the patronage of Ernst Ludwig, from an early photograph (Stadtarchiv, Darmstadt)

142 Joseph Maria Olbrich Haus, Darmstadt (Stadtarchiv, Darmstadt)

143 The opening of the Ernst Ludwig Haus at the beginning of the 1901 exhibition, 'A Document of German Art' (Stadtarchiv, Darmstadt)

One of the most exciting events at the exhibition was the judging of a competition for the design of 'A House for an Art Connoisseur', in which Baillie Scott's design *Dulce Domum* won the highest award, closely followed by C. R. Mackintosh against considerable continental competition. Baillie Scott introduced his entry with a characteristic Romantic manifesto:

In the mind of the artist, the art lover is one who ought to live in his house of dreams, not a man whose only qualification to this title rests with his connoisseurship . . . the true lover of art begins at the root of the problem: there should be no object in the house which is not the product of sympathetic human craftsmanship; the knives and forks, the glasses, the daily china, should all speak of the hopes and worries, the dreams and wishes of the creator.

42

43

Like so many architects, Baillie Scott is at his best in such dream buildings, unrealized in bricks and mortar, that reveal the most quintessential of his ideas. In 1903, in *The Studio* he published some plans for an imaginary sea-side house 'Yellowsands'. These strangely haunting designs, resemble an imaginative child's toy village and look forward to that most successful of twentieth-century follies, Clough William Ellis's 'Portmeirion'.

'Yellowsands' forms an appropriate point at which to terminate this brief discussion of Baillie Scott's work. He was to continue to play an important part in such enterprises as the building of Hampstead Garden Suburb and Letchworth Garden City, and indeed, unlike Voysey and Mackintosh, kept on building, though in less idiosyncratic style, until his retirement in 1939. For this he has not been forgiven, except by the Poet Laureate, Sir John Betjeman, and his admirable biographer James Kornwolf.

The diagonal axial scheme of Baillie Scott's *Dulce Domum* and its later even more fanciful variation 'Yellowsands', were echoed in the work of many continental architects, notably Leopold Bauer, Bruno Paul and Joseph Hoffmann in his famous design for the Stoclet House in Brussels (1905–1911). All these architects were led to their admiration and knowledge of such British designers as Baillie Scott, Lutyens, Voysey, Prior and Wood through reading the monumental work of Hermann Muthesius (1861–1927), the three volume *Das Englishe Haus* published in 1905. Muthesius, although himself an architect (his Freudenberg house near Berlin of 1907–8 also shows the tell-tale 'butterfly' lay-out of Baillie Scott), is notably remembered as a fervent exponent of the virtues of English design theories in Germany. In 1896 he had been sent to England, attached to the German Embassy, specifically to report on current developments in English architecture. So thoroughly was he to carry out his brief that his work remains the definitive account of the architecture of the period. The appointment reflects the considerable Teutonic interest in the English craft movement at this period, which also led to the founding by Joseph Hoffmann in 1903 of the Wiener Werkstätten modelled on C. R. Ashbee's Guild and School of Handicrafts, and similar groups in Munich, Dresden, Berlin and Hanover.

On his return to Germany, Muthesius was to play a leading part, together with members of these Werkstätten, in founding the Deutsche Werkbund in 1907, with the aim of 'selecting the best representatives of art, industry, crafts and trades, of combining all efforts towards high quality in industrial work, and of forming a rallying-point for all those who are able and willing to work for high quality'. Belief in 'quality' work did not preclude machine production, and in his inaugural address to the group, the architect Theodor Fischer echoed the words of William Morris . . . 'it is not the machines in themselves that make work inferior, but our inability to use them properly'.

After a few years of stormy and polemical argument, the Werkbund

144 Chair by Richard
Riemerschmidt, 1903 (Victoria
and Albert Museum)

succeeded, unlike the British Craft movement which had been its inspiration, in putting idealistic design theories into practice. It was able to do this, as from its foundation it had the advantage of national institutional and commercial support, unlike the characteristically ad hoc individualism of the relatively small-scale English ventures. Participants in the Werkbund's activities included such diverse figures as Richard Riemerschmidt, Peter Behrens, Gropius, and Henri Van de Velde, who had begun to work at Weimar in 1902, establishing an arts and crafts school there which was to become the Bauhaus. While the individual aims of such figures varied greatly, the exhibition of the Werkbund's productions in 1914 at Cologne was to vindicate its aims completely, and demonstrate that artistic aims could be integrated within a machine aesthetic.

These achievements were regarded with some suspicion by the founders of the English movement. In 1916, on the occasion of the Arts and Crafts Exhibition Society's big war-time show at the Royal Academy, the *Daily News* printed an interview with Henry Wilson, the Society's President, under the stirring headline, 'Art and Trade.— British Plans to Beat the Germans.—The Jam-Pot Beautiful'. In it he said, '. . . Foreigners . . . who make a study of these matters say . . . "we are enormously interested in your decorative art, because there you undoubtedly lead the world". Germany recognized that. Before the war she was actually in the habit of sending commissioners over here to crib our ideas and buy up our artists and craftsmen.' The interview sparked off a lively correspondence, which is worth quoting at some length. For Henry Marillier, reviewing the exhibition, the British show seemed too pretty. 'Individualism flourishes everywhere. The effect is spotty; but, after all spottiness is the hall mark of our national genius.' This review brought a howl of protest from R. B. Cunningham-Graham: 'Anyone who has seen the soulless productions of what the Germans refer to as "ard noufeau" at the Werkbund must be without artistic perception to compare them to the beautiful exhibits of William Morris and the great group of artists inspired by his example . . . Our soldiers and sailors may fight to free us from Prussian militarism, but the insidious propaganda of German commercialism seems to have some acceptation in London even yet'. More temperately Christopher Whall, the stained glass designer commented, 'The Germans "organize" and we "muddle through", but the net result of individuality, in arms as well as arts and industries, seems to be that when we have got in a hopeless tangle some mad genius always pops round the corner and does the impossible things . . . We need organisation,' he ends, 'all acknowledge it, but let us organize individuality'.

After the war, modern design found it had outgrown the need for such an avuncular approach. Houses for Art Lovers were no more the dominant need—what was wanted, to use the phrase of Le Corbusier, himself steeped in the traditions of the Deutsche Werkbund, were 'Machines for Living'.

145 Bedroom door by M. H.
Baillie Scott, *The Studio*,
April, 1899

7

Utopia Versus Reality: C. R. Ashbee's Guild Experiment and the Contemporary Situation

HARLES ROBERT ASHBEE was both the most successful and the most enigmatic exponent of the ideology of the Arts and Crafts Movement. We are puzzled and fascinated by his character, with its curious blend of practicality and Quixotic idealism. 'even the lecturer's pointer', it has been said of him, 'was held like a lance with which to tilt against the dragons'. While in some ways he represents the 'highest common denominator' of the movement's thought, what makes Ashbee so intriguing are the contradictions in his character, his non-socialist paternalism, his ability to write, late in life, an excellent book on *Caricature*. Above all, we find enigmatic the reasons for the success of his Cotswold venture, one of the most potent Arts and Crafts legends. We seek an explanation of the qualities that enabled him to lead, like a Pied-Piper, a hundred and fifty east-enders from the Mile End Road to the rural calm of Chipping Campden in Gloucestershire. What made him so different from other leading exponents of Arts and Crafts ideals?

Some answers to the complexity of his character are provided by his family background. He was born at Isleworth on May 17th, 1863, the only son of Henry Spencer Ashbee (1834–1900), and his wife Elisabeth Lavy of Hamburg. His father, a wealthy, much travelled merchant, formed the largest Victorian private collection of erotic literature and pornography, which he catalogued under the pseudonym, *Pisanus Fraxi*. If, as has been suggested, H. S. Ashbee was also the author of the anonymous classic of sexual literature, the extraordinarily revealing autobiography, *My Secret Life*, it easily explains the reason for the estrangement and eventual break up of C. R. Ashbee's parents' marriage. It is hardly surprising that Charles Robert Ashbee should grow up with an unconcealed dislike of his father and a corresponding deep affection for his mother, who brought him up with his sisters, standard ingredients for homosexual proclivities. These facts would be of only incidental interest had Ashbee, after a conventional education at Wellington and King's College, Cambridge (where he read history as a contemporary and friend of Roger Fry and Lowes Dickinson) not encountered Edward Carpenter, (1844–1929).

Carpenter, a friend of William Morris, the socialist Hyndman, and Walt Whitman, was originally a clergyman. In 1874 he abandoned Holy Orders and a Cambridge Fellowship to devote himself to University Extension lecturing at Leeds, Halifax and Skipton. In 1877 he visited Walt Whitman in America, and inspired by this contact, published in 1884 a long prose poem *Towards Democracy*. In this work he attacked the contemporary conditions of the labouring classes, advocated a return to the pastoral simplicity of life before the Industrial Revolution, and pleaded for a fuller appreciation of the English cultural heritage. All these aims, unexceptionable enough, were to be espoused by Ashbee with deep conviction throughout his life. He also, one can surmise, viewed with sympathy Carpenter's own original 'comradely' concern for the working man, expressed in such lines as these to a begrimed stoker:

146 Chipping Campden High Street in 1902, when C. R. Ashbee and fifty families from London's East End arrived by bicycle to begin the Guild experiment, from *Annual Report* of the Guild and School of Handicrafts

Well, as it happened just then—and as we stopped at a small way-station—my eyes from their swoon-sleep opening encountered the grimy and oil-besmeared figure of a stoker.

Close at my elbow on the foot-plate of his engine he was standing, devouring bread and cheese,

And the firelight fell on him brightly as for a moment his eyes rested on mine. That was all. But it was enough.

It is not merely prurient to comment upon this male oriented strand in the complex visionary background of the movement. For Whitman and Carpenter their homosexual proclivities found expression in a sincere concern for the lot of the working class man which can aptly be described as a more passionate version of William Morris's belief in Fellowship, as expressed in *The Dream of John Ball*: 'Forsooth, brothers, fellowship is heaven, and lack of fellowship is hell: fellowship is life, and lack of fellowship is death . . .'

For Ashbee in 1886, just down from University and articled to the architect G. F. Bodley, these teachings provided a novel and stimulating alternative to the trammelled confines of a predictable upper-middle class professional career. His contact, during the next fifteen years of his life, with the working classes of the East End, gave him just the insight into poverty which he needed to make him accepted as an idealist with some grasp of reality.

148 Essex House, in the Mile
End Road, the frontispiece to
*An Endeavour Towards the
Teachings of John Ruskin and
William Morris*

During the years he spent in Bodley's office, Ashbee lived at the Universities Settlement at Toynbee Hall in Whitechapel. Roger Fry lived there also, and for some years helped Ashbee with his educational activities in the evenings. It heightens our picture of their activities to remember that while Ashbee read and discussed Ruskin's *Fors Clavigera* and *Crown of Wild Olive* with the local men and boys, Jack the Ripper perpetrated his terrible murders within a mile of the lecture hall. The unreality of the Settlement's educational efforts had an incongruity which was not lost on Ashbee, who felt that Toynbee Hall, though well intentioned, was on the wrong lines, 'neither a college, convent nor a club'. Something more practical was needed, and he began to teach drawing and decoration, finding a responsive audience in men chained to uncongenial and repetitive jobs. From these beginnings emerged Ashbee's solution of a 'cooperative' of skilled craftsmen united in a Guild, each man playing a responsible part in its affairs and helping to run a School in conjunction with the Guild, where young apprentices could be trained by the Guildsmen in their chosen crafts.

Fired with enthusiasm Ashbee, then aged twenty-four, went to see William Morris at Hammersmith on December 4th, 1887. On his return to Toynbee Hall he wrote in his journal: 'William Morris and a great deal of cold water! Spent last evening with him,—by appointment,—à propos of "Art Schools". He says it is useless, and that I am about to do a thing with no basis to do it on. I anticipated all he said to me ... I could not exchange a single argument with him until I granted his whole position as a Socialist and then said: "Look, I am going to forge a weapon for you;—and thus I too work for you in the overthrow of Society". To which he replied, "The weapon is too small to be of any value".' Despite this declaration to Morris, Ashbee was never a socialist, and his control of the Guild was always, from both the design and administrative points of view, virtually absolute, although in theory the Guildsmen were required to learn the art of design themselves.

Undeterred by this and other discouragements, both Guild and School of Handicrafts came into being a few months later on June 23rd, 1888, the opening at Toynbee Hall being graced by the President of the Board of Education, and the new Guild shortly afterwards being given the accolade of a lecture from Morris. Amazingly, the new enterprise thrived and soon moved from Toynbee Hall, first to the top floor of a warehouse nearby, and then to Essex House, a handsome Georgian house in the Mile End Road, at the same time opening a shop in the West End at 16a Brook Street.

At Essex House, carpentry, carving, cabinet making and decorative painting were carried on, but the main emphasis came more and more to be placed on metalwork. A smithy was built in the garden, and silver-work, enamelling and, increasingly, jewellery became valued aspects of the Guild's work. Probably while working for G. F. Bodley, Ashbee had acquired a deep knowledge of English plate, which in the early 1890s he

147 Oak cabinet, painted in red and gold, inscribed with quotations from *The Auguries of Innocence* by William Blake (Abbotsholme School, Rochester, Staffordshire)

126

AN ENDEAVOUR TOWARDS THE TEACH~ING OF JOHN RUSKIN AND WILLIAM MORRIS.

BEING A BRIEF ACCOUNT OF THE WORK, THE AIMS, AND THE PRINCIPLES OF THE GUILD OF HANDICRAFT IN EAST LON~DON, WRITTEN BY C. R. ASHBEE, AND DEDICATED BY HIM LESS IN THE WRIT~ING, THAN IN THE WORK THE WRITING SEEKS TO SET FORTH, TO THEIR MEM~ORY. AN. DOM. MDCCCCI.

149

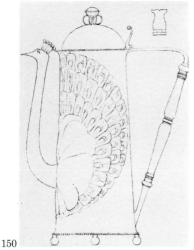

150

149 Four pieces of early Guild and School of Handicraft metalwork

150 Illustration of Peacock coffee pot from *Modern British Silverwork* by C. R. Ashbee

supplemented by the study of Benvenuto Cellini's treatise on goldsmithing. This knowledge, deepened by constant experimentation at the bench with his craftsmen, led to the relatively rapid evolution of a distinctive Guild style, elegant, eclectic yet highly original. A marked feature of the Guild's productions, almost from the first, was the imaginative use of multiple wire threads, enamelling and semi-precious stones.

Throughout the 1890s Ashbee was an intensely busy man, maintaining an architectural practice, founding what was to become the Survey of London, and playing an active part in the foundation of the National Trust. But despite these activities he began to dream more and more of establishing a real rural community of craftsmen. A Guildsman, H. Phillips, a carpenter, conducted a short-lived 'Country Centre' of the Guild at the progressive school for boys at Abbotsholme in Staffordshire in the early 1890s. Weekend country cottages were set up to enable the Guildsmen, apprentices and their families to get together, in Essex, Middlesex, Buckinghamshire and Oxfordshire. Ashbee felt that these weekends 'helped no little to unite our people and give us the right taste for the country'. He goes on, 'I seem to see in the prevalent fashion of the weekend cottage the beginning of the decentralization of industry which is to destroy the great town. Not a few of the little Arts and Crafts in this way have gone into the country . . .'

The enterprise had, of course, its ups and downs. The School failed for lack of funds in 1895, despite Ashbee's appeal to the L.C.C. for help. But although inevitably frequently hard-pressed for money, the Guild's work became widely known through exhibitions, both at home, at Arts and Crafts exhibitions in London and the provinces, and internationally. Much publicity was given to the decoration by the Guild of Ashbee's own Chelsea house 'The Magpie and Stump', by long articles in *The Studio* magazine in 1895, and by Herman Muthesius in *Dekoratif Kunst* in 1898. This was the welcome publicity which led Ernst Ludwig, Grand Duke of Hesse, to commission the architect M. H. Ballie Scott to decorate the Grand Duke's palace, the design being carried out by the Guild.

The year 1898 was indeed an important one for Ashbee in many ways. He married Janet Elizabeth Forbes, an accomplished musician, who worked devotedly to further the Guild idea, playing the leading part in the musical evenings which became a feature of the Guild's activities. These evenings are commemorated in the *Essex House Song Book*. This book, originally issued as separate sheets, was one of the most delightful productions of the Essex House Press which also came into being in 1898, when Ashbee acquired from William Morris's Trustees the stock and plant of the Kelmscott Press.

The Morris Trustees withheld the fount and cuts, but Ashbee would almost certainly, in any case, have wanted to do something original. There were however, honoured links with Kelmscott, both in machines—the two Albion presses Morris had used—and in men: Binning, the Kelmscott Press compositor, Hooper and Catterson-Smith, who had adapted Burne-Jones' drawings into woodcuts, came to Essex House. The Press's publications enabled Ashbee both to explore new fields of typography and to publicize the work of the Guild in such works as *An Endeavour Towards the Teachings of William Morris and John Ruskin* of 1901. A delightful feature of many of the books is Ashbee's own initial letters, particularly the Alphabet illustrated (Fig. 151),

151 'Alphabet of Pinks' designed by C. R. Ashbee, and used in the Essex House Press publications, inspired by the pinks that grew in the garden of Essex House

152 Initial letter T encircling the tower of Chipping Campden parish church by C. R. Ashbee

which uses the pink (*Dianthus*) emblem of the Guild, weaving the flowers and foliage through the letter forms, in a way which, though reminiscent of Morris, is highly imaginative.

The year 1898 was also marked by Ashbee's decision to turn the Guild into a limited company, each Guildsman being granted shares according to the length of his service.

In 1900 Ashbee became aware that the lease on Essex House had only two years left to run. He wrote later in *Craftsmanship in Competitive Industry*, 1908:

We searched in the great town to see whether we could find there a suitable place for our new workshops. We tried Mile End and Bow, South Byfleet and the eastern districts, we tried Fulham & Chelsea and Putney and Brompton, we went north and tried Ruislip and Harrow. None of these for one reason or another seemed good enough, until we went right out into the little forgotten Cotswold town of the Age of Arts and Crafts where industrialism had never touched, where there was an old mill and empty cottages ready to hand, left almost as when the Arts and Crafts ended in the 18th century.

While the decision to move to Chipping Campden was theoretically a democratic one, Ashbee conducting a poll among Guild members, there can be little doubt that it was his enthusiasm for Campden that was the determining factor. Morris and De Morgan had also felt the attraction of the idyllic village before they established their premises at Merton, but had felt that it was too far from London. While Ashbee's experience was to prove Morris and De Morgan right, it is impossible not to be moved by the mental picture of the young apprentices on their bicycles, like H. G. Wells' Kipps, freewheeling down the Cotswold hills into the golden lanes of what remains to this day one of England's most beautiful places.

The move to Campden of fifty families, a hundred and fifty people in all, has often been described, but never fails to appeal to the imagination, since it has the Utopian glamour of all lost causes. Ashbee, fired with the beauty of the dilapidated cottages of an area hit by agricultural depression, embarked on an intensive programme of restoration. F. L. M. Grigg's etchings, originally published in the Guild's annual reports, sensitively record Izod's cottage seen both from the High Street, Campden, and the garden, and the Island House or Middle Row, Campden which was used in part as the Craftsman Club, in part as the bindery of the Guild; while E. H. New's woodcut shows the old malthouse converted into the Campden School of Arts and Crafts, its interior suitably inscribed with such appropriate mottoes as 'The Lyf so short, The Craft so Longe to Lerne'.

Here Ashbee grasped briefly the ideal opportunity to extend the educational aspects of his work, organizing Oxford University extension classes and summer schools, and persuading his friends like Walter Crane to talk on *Design in Relation to the Crafts*, and Edward Carpenter on *Small Holdings and Life on the Land*. All would have been

153 *Izod's cottage, front view*, woodcut by F. L. Griggs from the *Annual Report* of the Guild and School of Handicrafts, 1905

154 *Izod's cottage, rear view*, woodcut by F. L. Griggs

155 *Island House, or Middle Row*, woodcut by F. L. Griggs

156 *Chipping Campden School of Arts and Crafts*, woodcut by E. H. New from the Guild's *Annual Report*, 1905

130

153

154

155

156

131

well had he stopped at this, but Ashbee's quixotic wish to teach the local people 'skills such as are not provided in the Campden Elementary Schools' led him into difficulties:

We have been visited in five years by eleven different inspectors, many of them overlapping, and giving conflicting instructions, we have to do annually with more than fifteen separate educational authorities, we have to fill innumerable forms . . . all for the sake of an annual grant of £150 . . . and all this rigmarole, all this pishery-pashery before public money may be used in teaching a little girl to wash an apron or a village lad to use an anvil, not to mention some trifle of music or national literature, as a palliative to the maudlin sentiment of the parish magazine, or the uncontrolled rubbish of the cheap press.

But if life for the educational reformer in Campden itself had its difficulties, within the Guild Ashbee's ideas could have free play. For the Guildsmen and their families performances of Shakespeare, Jonson and Dekker alternated with brass band practice, swimming galas, domestic science lessons and physical jerks in what must have been a stimulating if exhausting daily round. Much stress was naturally laid on tilling the soil, and the Guild's reports show jewellery and silversmithing produced by craftsmen engaged upon their own tillage. Four examples from their productions must suffice here to indicate their range. Ashbee's designs for nut crackers (Fig. 161), using the favourite Arts and Crafts device of squirrels; a brooch in silver in the form of a proud peacock set with opals and mother of pearl (Fig. 165); a chalice of 1903 (Fig. 163), the form inspired by an Elizabethan communion cup; and a standing cup and cover (Fig. 164), the elegant stem contrasting with the *repoussée* swellings inspired by late 16th-century German so-called 'pineapple' cups. The whole Campden exercise has a surprisingly Russian flavour, reminiscent of the ideas of Tolstoy, and in the instructor's plot and craftsmen's plots anticipating the example of the Stakhanovite worker.

157 Gymnastic classes held for members of the Guild and School of Handicrafts

158 'Jewellery produced by craftsmen engaged upon their own tillage', from the *Annual Report*, 1906

159 Instructor's plot and Craftsmen's plots. *Annual Report*, 1906

160 Craftsmen engaged upon their own tillage, *Annual Report* of the Guild and School of Handicrafts, 1906

157

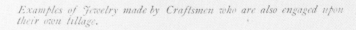

158

High Road.

gate

Yew
○ Tree

| Plot 1. |
| Plot 2. |
| Plot 3. |
| Plot 4. |
| Plot 5. |
| Plot 6. |
| Plot 7. |
| Plot 8. |
| Plot 9. |
| Plot 10. |
| Plot 11. |
| Plot 12. |
| The Instructor's Plot. |

For Experimental Fruit.

Path.

Boundary Wall.

gate

School
buildings

Examples of Jewelry made by Craftsmen who are also engaged upon their own tillage.

160

161 Design for nut crackers
by C. R. Ashbee (Victoria and
Albert Museum)

162 Soup tureen, cover and
ladle, silver plated copper and
brass, designed by C. R.
Ashbee and made by the Guild
and School of Handicrafts,
c. 1890

163 Chalice for Broad
Campden Parish Church, 1903
(Victoria and Albert Museum)

164 'The painter-stainer's cup'
in silver set with semi-
precious stones, *c.* 1900, by
C. R. Ashbee (Victoria and
Albert Museum)

165 Peacock Brooch in silver
set with opals and mother of
pearl by C. R. Ashbee
(Victoria and Albert Museum)

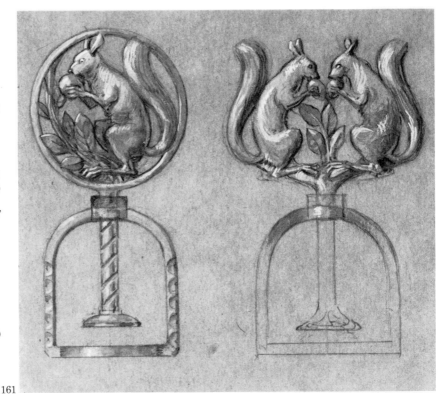

161

162

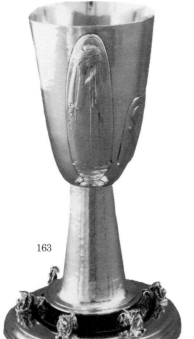

163

Given all these excitements it is surprising that the Guild managed to continue to produce work which was still internationally acclaimed. However some Guild furniture exhibited at one of the Vienna Secession exhibitions appeared to an Austrian critic 'like pieces of brown bread after a Lucullan repast, as if they came from a square planet inhabited by stout built peasants, everything upright, angular at 90 degrees, English Biedermeir, plain, strong and heavy'.

This rural idyll unfortunately lasted for only six years. Communications, as expected, proved the difficulty. The delays and losses involved in transmitting orders to the country from the expensive retail premises in Bond Street proved too great for the Guild to bear, and it went into voluntary liquidation in 1908. Ashbee managed to persuade a friend Joseph Fels to finance a scheme for those craftsmen who decided to remain at Chipping Campden by buying 70 acres of land, thus enabling the Guildsmen to supplement their craft earnings by agricultural work.

In his conclusion to *Craftsmanship in Competitive Industry*, his history of the Chipping Campden venture, Ashbee wrote: 'As for the immediate readjustment of the little undertaking . . . it is but an episode in the greater movement of the Arts and Crafts in Modern Industry . . . what does it matter! When the heap of ants is overturned, there is momentary confusion, and then the pile begins again.'

Ashbee's natural feelings of disillusioned fatalism at the relative failure of his experiment must be placed in perspective. A true assessment of the value of the Guild venture can only be made if its achievements are contrasted with the prevailing attitudes to craftsmanship at the time. These attitudes differed widely, and it is rewarding to examine them in some depth by using contemporary quotations from writers working during the years that saw the emergence and eclipse of the Guild venture.

A salutary knowledge of what life was really like for the majority of urban workmen and craftsmen can be gained from the pages of Robert Tressell's famous novel *The Ragged Trousered Philanthropists*. It gives a vivid picture of the realities of life as experienced by many of the members of the Guild before they joined Ashbee's venture.

'Robert Tressell' was the pseudonym adopted by Robert Noonan (1871–1911). He was himself one of the workmen he describes, wrote the book in his spare time, and knew exactly what he was talking about. The novel, published in 1911, describes the life of a group of painters and decorators in Hastings (Mugsborough) in 1906. Here is his description of the foreman, Hunter, nicknamed 'Nimrod' or 'Misery':

When an estimate was to be prepared it was Hunter who measured up the work and laboriously figured out the probable cost. When their tenders were accepted it was he who superintended the work and schemed how to scamp it, where possible, using mud where mortar was specified, mortar where there ought to have been cement, sheet zinc where there was supposed to be sheet lead, boiled

166 Herkomer's *On Strike* of 1883, his Diploma painting for the Royal Academy. The work reflects the widespread concern for the labouring classes shared by figures as diverse as Cardinal Manning and William Morris, who both played a part in the industrial dispute which inspired this picture, 'the strike for the docker's tanner' (Royal Academy of Arts)

oil instead of varnish, and three coats of paint where five were paid for. In fact, scamping the work was with this man a kind of mania. It grieved him to see anything done properly. Even when it was more economical to do a thing well, he insisted from force of habit on having it scamped. Then he was almost happy, because he felt he was doing someone down.

In practice, Hunter's aims were sometimes thwarted by an odd phenomenon—the skilled workman's pride in his job. But Nimrod had his own ways of dealing with this problem. In the following passage he discusses a workman called Newman, with his toady, the potential foreman, Crass:

I've 'ad me eye on 'im for some time . . . Anybody would think the work was goin' to be sent to a Exhibition, the way 'e messes about with it, rubbing it with glasspaper and stopping up every little crack! I can't understand where 'e gets all the glasspaper *from*!

"E brings it 'isself!' said Crass hoarsely. 'I know for a fact that 'e bought two a'penny sheets of it, last week, out of 'is own money!'

Misery, enraged, seeks out Newman:

[He] found him alone in one of the upper rooms, to which he was giving the final coat. He was at his old tricks. The woodwork on the cupboard he was doing was in a rather damaged condition, and he was facing up the dents with white-lead putty before painting it. He knew quite well that Hunter objected to any but very large holes or cracks being stopped, and yet somehow or other he could not scamp the work to the extent that he was ordered to; and so, almost by stealth, he was in the habit of doing it—not properly—but as well as he dared. He even went to the lengths of occasionally buying a few sheets of glasspaper with his own money, as Crass has told Hunter. When the latter came into the room he stood with a sneer on his face, watching Newman for about five minutes before he spoke. The workman became very nervous and awkward under this scrutiny.

'You can make out yer time-sheet and come to the office for yer money at five o'clock', said Nimrod at last. 'We shan't require your valuable services no more after tonight.'

Newman went white.

'Why, what's wrong?' said he. 'What have I done?'

'Oh, it's not wot you've *done*', replied Misery. 'It's wot you've *not* done. That's wot's wrong! You've not done enough, that's all!' . . . 'My God!' said Newman, realizing the almost utter hopelessness of the chance of obtaining another 'job' and unconsciously speaking aloud. 'My God! . . . What *will* become of us!'

This incident, which has the ring of absolute veracity, was no isolated phenomenon. But if men could be exploited, women were even more vulnerable. The inhuman system of 'sweating', which arose out of the common practice of allowing certain types of skilled hand work to be carried out in people's homes, enabled the foreman, forewoman or sub-contractor to offer the lowest possible rates of pay for the maximum amount of work. In the same year that Tressel's novel was written, in

May, 1906, a widely publicized *Daily News* Sweated Industries Exhibition was held at the Central Hall, Westminster, organized with the support of Mr. and Mrs. Ramsay Macdonald and George Bernard Shaw.

The exhibition consisted of a number of stands at which outworkers demonstrated the work they did, while placards displayed the pitiful rates they obtained for their labours. It was an act of considerable courage for these workers to appear in this way, because they knew that they risked the possibility of being placed on a black list by their employers. To preserve their anonymity, numbers instead of names were used. Here are the brutal statistics of the lives of numbers 19 and 20, who were employed at the skilled work of sewing ornamental beadwork decoration on the elaborate costumes and shoes of Edwardian ladies dress:

Stall X	Worker No. 19	Worker No. 20
Description of Work	*Vamp beading on ladies' shoes*	*Beaded ornaments*
Rates paid	1s 7d—2s 6d per dozen pairs	2½d.—3½d. per dozen according to size
Worker's outlay for threads, etc.	2d. weekly. Finds own needles	1½d. weekly
Time lost in fetching and returning work	None	About 3 hours weekly
Average working day	14 hours	12 hours
Average earnings	6s 0d. weekly	5s 0d. weekly at most
Regular or intermittent work	Slack time June to December	6 months in year only
Worker's rent	3s 0d.	
Number of rooms	One	
Process	Each bead has to be put on separately by hand.	The worker has first to cut out the buckram, bind it, & put on the sequins & beads, each one separately. The work is bad for the eyes.
Remarks	This is an experienced worker who can do high class work	This worker has two small children dependent on her. Three others are in work but can allow her very little. Has had 'to pawn things to make ends meet'. Husband, an old man, helps his wife, & between them they can earn 7s 0d. per week.

For such workers, the Biblical phrase 'the labourer is worthy of his hire' became a hollow mockery, and Ruskin's term 'slaves' was an entirely accurate description of their lot. For Newman and No. 19, craftsmanship *was* more than a mere theoretical issue. For men like Tressel, Arts and Crafts theories alone could not suffice, without closely related activist socialist programmes, to improve the worker's lot. Ashbee's Guild and School of Handicrafts had shown that there was an alternative to the sweat shop, and enabled a few, at least, to escape from the city to the country. There, in some measure, jerrybuilding and sweating were not the universal pattern, and pride could be taken in work well done without the fear of the sack.

How different, for example, is the foreman described in the following passage by the great gardener Gertrude Jekyll (1843–1932) in her book *Home and Garden*, published in 1900. In it she describes the pleasure she took in watching her house, designed by Sir Edwin Lutyens, built:

167 *Gertrude Jekyll's Gardening Boots* by William Nicholson, 1920 (Tate Gallery)

How I enjoy seeing the whole operation of the building from its very beginning! I could watch any clever workman for hours. Even the shovelling and shaping of

ground is pleasant to see, but when it comes to a craftsman of long experience using the tool that seems to have become a part of himself, the attraction is so great that I can hardly tear myself away. What a treat it was to see the foreman building a bit of wall! . . . How good it was to observe the absolute precision, the perfect command of the tool and material; to see the ease of it, the smiling face, the rapid, almost dancing movements, the exuberant, though wholly unaffected manifestation of ready activity; the little graceful ornaments of actions in half-unconscious flourishes of the trowel, delicate fioriture of consummate dexterity, and all looking so pleasantly easy that the movements seemed less those of a man plying his trade than such as one sees in a strong young creature frisking for very pleasure in glad life.

. . . How well I got to know all the sounds! The chop and rush of the trowel taking up its load of mortar from the board, the dull slither as the moist mass was laid as a bed for the next brick in the course; the ringing music of the soft-tempered blade cutting a well-burnt brick, the muter tap of its shoulder settling it into its place, aided by the down-bearing pressure of the finger tips of the left hand; the sliding scrape of the tool taking up the overmuch mortar that squeezed out of the joint, and the neat slapping of it into the cross-joint . . . the rhythmical sound of the shovel in the sloppy mortar as it turned over and over to incorporate the lime and sand.

This lyrical passage is only one of many by Gertrude Jekyll, who had an unerring eye for noting down the rhythm of rural craftsmanship. In her delightful book *Wood and Garden*, published in 1899, she describes the art of thatching:

I got a clever old thatcher to make me a hoop-chip roof for the garden shed; it was a long job, and he took his time (although it was piece work) preparing and placing each handful of chips as carefully as if he were making a wedding bouquet. He was one of the old sort—no scamping of work for him; his work was as good as he could make it, and it was his pride and delight. The roof was prepared with strong laths nailed horizontally across the rafters as if for tiling but farther apart; and the chips, after a number of handfuls had been duly placed and carefully poked and patted into shape, were bound down to the laths with soft tarred cord guided by an immense iron needle. The thatching, as in all cases of roof covering, begins at the eaves, so that each following layer laps over the last. Only the ridge has to be of straw, because straw can be bent over; the chips are too rigid. When the thatch is all in place the whole is 'drove', that is, beaten up close with a wooden bat that strikes against the end of the chips and drives them up close, jamming them tight into the fastening. After six months of drying summer weather, he came and drove it all over again.

Gertrude Jekyll's felicity in observing the rhythm of rural crafts was to find a perfect visual counterpart, many years later, in the sensitive line engravings of Stanley Anderson (1884–1966).

In these quotations are mirrored the two opposed aspects of life at the turn of the nineteenth century, against which Ashbee's activities must be

set. Like Thomas Hardy, he regretted the passing of the old tight-knit rural communities in which the crafts could flourish and the parallel expansion of the urban ant-heap with its shoddier standards. Despite his own personal disillusionment, it is heartening to record that some of the craftsmen left at Chipping Campden after the winding up of the Guild's activities succeeded in remaining there and having productive later careers, notably the silversmith George Hart. But Ashbee's own life and his personal attitudes to the continuing Arts and Crafts struggle against modern industrialism were to undergo considerable changes. His friendship with Frank Lloyd Wright, author of *The Arts and Crafts of the Machine*, led to a modification of Ashbee's attitudes, reflected in such publications as *Shall we stop teaching Art?* of 1911, which contains a radically different statement of aims: 'Modern civilization rests on machinery, and no system of endowment, or the encouragement, or the teaching of art can be sound that does not recognise this.'

From 1915 until 1923 Ashbee worked in the Middle East, latterly in the Holy Land, where, for the Palestine administration, by whom he was employed as Civic Advisor, he undertook the Blakean challenge of devising plans for the improvement of Jerusalem. Although he was to continue to maintain a lively interest in the crafts, becoming Master of the Art Workers' Guild in 1929, his later years, spent in retirement at Godden Green near Sevenoaks, were devoted, surprisingly, to the production of an excellent book on caricature. He died on May 23rd, 1942.

Ashbee's vision was a remarkable one, and although his Utopia failed, it would be wrong to regard him as merely the most successful crank in a cranky movement. In his book *Where the Great City Stands*, written during the First World War, and published in 1917, he outlined his hopes for post-war society, in an appeal to the Practical Idealist. In it he printed a series of axioms, notably these:

Axiom VI. The distinction between what should and what should not be produced by machinery has in many trades and crafts now been made. This has been the discovery of the last twenty-five years.

Axiom X. In an industrial civilization, the reconstructed city cannot be stable without a corresponding reconstruction of the country. Town and country should be correlated and react upon one another. This correlation is a natural consequence of the conditions of machine industry.

It would be hard to think of two statements which better anticipate our own contemporary attitudes to these questions.

The book also contains his unrealized plan for The Ruislip Garden City, with its Palladian bridge over a railway, cooperative settlements, and prominent use of the term 'The Green Belt'. Although Ashbee's attempts to put these plans into effect failed, they remind us again of the Whitman-esque social ideals which he and his friend Edward Carpenter shared:

168 Stanley Anderson's line engraving, *Windsor Chairs* (Fine Art Society)

The place where a great city stands . . .

. . . is not the place of the most numerous population

. . . where equanimity is illustrated in affairs

. . . where speculations on the soul are encouraged

. . . There the great city stands.

169 Ruislip Garden City, from *Where the Great City Stands*, 1917

Such principles continue to have a lasting validity while cities such as Milton Keynes are developed.

RUISLIP GARDEN CITY

8

The Arts and
Crafts
in America

S WE HAVE SEEN, the origins of the Arts and Crafts Movement in Great Britain sprang from the teachings and examples of Pugin, Carlyle, Ruskin and William Morris, all in their differing ways concerned with the dangerous impact of industrial development on modern society, and advocating a return to the ideal craft Utopia and social structure of a mediaeval world.

The genesis of the American movement was of a very different nature. The emergent American nation admired, rather than deplored, the power of industry to provide energy and the means to establish a new and vital society. Yet while the machine was seen as an ally, rather than a foe, the classic American virtues of independence and self-sufficiency, and belief in the value of close contact with nature, found many differing voices. These voices ranged from the electioneering slogan proclaiming the right of every citizen to 'ten acres and a cow', to the complete expression of the emergent national consciousness in Whitman's *Leaves of Grass*, much of which was written during the 1850s while the poet maintained himself by working as carpenter and builder.

These ideas, as we have seen, had found sympathetic auditors in England in the 1880s. Ashbee gained from his friendship with Edward Carpenter, 'the English Whitman', a deep appreciation of *Leaves of Grass*, and selected from it the text of 'Where the Great City Stands' for an early publication of the Essex House Press. Its words might almost be said to be the inspirational expression of the ideas which led Ashbee to found the Guild and School of Handicrafts and place it in its rural setting in the Cotswolds.

Again and again in reading Whitman the aptness of his writings to an Arts and Crafts context strikes deep. In the following passage from his notes on writing *Leaves of Grass*, his choice of similes, 'a bird flying', 'a fish swimming', are dynamic and natural, and significantly anticipate some of the most frequently used motifs of artists of the movement as diverse as Mackmurdo and Henry Wilson. 'Lumber the writing with nothing—let it go as lightly as the bird flies in the air or a fish swims in the sea. Avoid all poetical similes; be faithful to the perfect likelihoods of nature—healthy, exact, simple, disdaining ornaments ...' advice which might almost stand as an Arts and Crafts basic design manual. It was these qualities in Whitman which gave his words their potent appeal in England, where the natural expression of new ideas so often takes a poetic or literary form.

The truth of the old phrase that a prophet is without honour in his own country comes to mind when the influence of the writings of Emerson, Thoreau and Whitman is evaluated on the emergent craft movement in the United States. This is hardly surprising. Their teachings were, after all, poetic and ecological, rather than with direct reference to the craft dilemma, the constantly reiterated concern of Carlyle, Ruskin and Morris. It was these concerns which were to begin to preoccupy American attention in the 1870s.

An important event in this process was the 1876 Centennial exhibition

170 *The Good Grey Poet: Walt Whitman*, woodcuts by Edward Gordon Craig from *The Portfolio*

Walt Whitman, October 20th, 1876.— "A clear crispy day, dry and breezy air full of oxygen. Out of the sane silent beauteous miracles that envelope and fuse me—trees, water, grass, sunlight, and early frost—the one I am looking at most to-day is the sky. It has that delicate transparent blue, peculiar to autumn, and the only clouds are little or larger white ones, giving their still and spiritual motion to the great concave. All through the earlier day (say from 7 to 11) it keeps a pure yet vivid blue. But as noon approaches the color gets lighter, quite gray for two or three hours—then still paler for a spell till sundown— which last I watch dazzling through the interstices of a knoll of big trees— darts of fire and a gorgeous show, light yellow, liver-color and red, with a vast silver glaze askant on the water — the transparent shadows, shafts, sparkle, and vivid colors beyond all the paintings ever made."

146

Stables, Wentworth Hall, Jackson, N.H.—Mr. W. A. Bates, Architect.

171 W. A. Bates, 'Stables', Jackson, New Hampshire, *The Builder*, 1889

at Philadelphia. Designed to celebrate a century of independence, the exhibition, in artistic terms, actually underlined the dependence of American taste on the more showy aspects of the prevailing international 'Exhibition' fashion for elaborate and flashy decoration. A sense of lack of direction in the development of the applied arts in America was keenly felt.

A key figure who emerges as a trans-Atlantic link at this time was the architect H. H. Richardson (1838–1886), whose adoption of the 'Queen Anne' style of Norman Shaw was to align avant-garde American taste with British developments. But Richardson's role was not that of plagiarist, but of broker. The exchange of architectural ideas was not only one-way. American domestic architecture of the period, particularly the work being done on the north-east sea-board, which has been described as 'the Shingle style', had a fresh and vernacular quality which echoed the enthusiasm of William Morris for the secular tithe barns of the middle ages. The English trade magazine *The Builder* published illustrations and articles about American architecture as early as 1875, and the study of such works as W. A. Bates' 'Stables', in Jackson, New Hampshire, published in *The Builder* in 1889, was to play an important part in the stylistic evolution of English architects such as Voysey, Lutyens and especially Baillie Scott.

The Shingle style was but one expression of the American dream of rural simplicity. As a life style, the simple life, pursued with religious fervour, had been a recurrent phenomenon in America from the time of the Pilgrim Fathers to the Shaker Communities of Kentucky and elsewhere, whose furniture has such obvious Arts and Crafts parallels.

147

172

172, 173 Two Shaker interiors from Shakertown, Pleasant Hill, Kentucky (photos: Jan Arnow)

174

The austere world of the Shakers had been a national curiosity since the late eighteenth century. It became widely known after its exhibition in the 1876 Centennial show at Philadelphia. The plain severity of its furniture made a direct appeal to a young man who visited the exhibition, who was to become one of the leading exponents of Arts and Crafts ideals in America, Gustav Stickley (1857–1942). The oldest of six brothers born in Osceola, Wisconsin, Stickley trained as a young man as a stonemason, a fact which may explain the monumental quality in much of his later 'Mission' furniture. Some of his earliest ventures in furniture making, in partnership with his brothers, took place at Binghampton, New York State. In his own words, 'We had no money to buy machinery. I went to a maker of broom handles who had a good turning lathe . . . and with it blocked out the plainest parts of some very simple chairs made after the "Shaker" model . . . The very primitiveness of the equipment, made necessary by lack of means, furnished what was really a golden opportunity to break away from the monotony of commercial forms'.

Although deeply influenced by the writings of John Ruskin, Stickley at first found it very difficult to escape from the economic demands for eclectic copies of colonial furniture. It was not until 1898 that he managed to establish an independent workshop at Syracuse, where his original ideas could find full expression. In the same year he visited Europe and met C. F. A. Voysey, Cobden-Sanderson and other designers in London, and Bing and leading Art Nouveau figures in Paris.

On his return to America he began to produce the severe, massive, aggressively simple oak pieces which became widely known and imitated as 'Mission' furniture—a fanciful term derived from an imagined

175

176

177

resemblance to the furniture produced by the Spanish seventeenth-century founders of missions in California. He adopted a trade name, 'Craftsman', and a device—a joiner's compass with the words *Alsik Kan*, which derived from Van Eyck, via William Morris. He renamed his company 'The United Crafts', organized his workshops on Guild lines and introduced a profit sharing plan for his workmen. In 1901 he began to publish the magazine *The Craftsman*, which was to run for sixteen years until its demise in 1916 after his bankruptcy. The magazine covered all the decorative arts, ranging widely over such subjects as William Morris, John Ruskin, the mediaeval guilds, to the work of René Lalique (whom Stickley had met in Paris at Bing's), the Garden City and Red Indian art—a favourite theme. The magazine became both an extremely effective advertizing vehicle and a forum of great importance for spreading Arts and Crafts ideas. In it, Stickley wrote of his 'Craftsman' furniture, 'When I first began to use the severely plain, structural form, I chose oak as the wood that, above all others, was adapted to massive simplicity of construction. The strong, straight lines and plain surfaces of the furniture follow and emphasize the grain and growth of the wood, drawing attention to, instead of destroying, the natural character that belonged to the growing tree . . .'

The resemblance of many of the pieces to the productions of the exactly contemporary Cotswold School on the other side of the Atlantic is striking. Stickley had met Lethaby on his visit to London in 1898, and it is hard to believe that Ernest Gimson and Sidney Barnsley could have been completely without knowledge of 'Craftsman' furniture, although their own productions have a subtle sophistication which is not found in the American pieces. On closer examination the differences are more profound than the resemblances. Stickley's frankly avowed aim was to produce 'democratic' furniture in his large works, using the circular saw to produce the effect of sharp angularity that proclaimed the unashamed use of the machine. Such aims were very different from those of the far smaller Cotswold group of craftsmen, who produced individually commissioned high quality artifacts.

Stickley's attempt to harness Arts and Crafts simplicity with his own modification of machine technology to produce a distinctive American furniture style commands respect. His magazine *The Craftsman* remains an eloquent and informative testimony to the concerns of the Arts and Crafts movement in America. But unfortunately both these ventures, and his attempt to set up a model farm and community in New Jersey, were to fail because of his miscalculated optimism in purchasing the twelve-storied skyscraper, 'The Craftsman Building', on Fifth Avenue in New York in 1913, at a time when public taste was beginning to react against the Arts and Crafts movement. His bankruptcy led to the collapse of the Craftsman empire in 1915 and his last years were spent in retirement.

If Stickley's character exemplifies the rugged American virtues of simplicity combined with enthusiasm, his immediate contemporary and

178 The United Craftsmen
furniture makers at work
rush-seating chairs

179 Writing desk and chair,
Stickley Brothers Company,
Grand Rapids, Michigan, 1906.
Gustav Stickley's younger
brothers, George and Albert,
founded an independent
company in 1891, whose
furniture paralleled that of
their brother and the
Cotswold school. They used
the words 'quaint furniture'
and 'Arts and Crafts' as
descriptive of their
productions (Art Museum,
Princeton University)

179

rival Elbert Hubbard (1856–1915) brings to the reticent world of the Arts and Crafts movement a refreshingly brash, P. T. Barnum showmanship. Hubbard was a born entrepreneur who started life as a soap salesman. He specialized in promotional offers—'Sweet Home soap at 6 dollars a box, with about 10 dollars worth of napkin rings, picture books, coffee spoons, baby rattles, wall pockets, men's neckties and Chautauqua desks thrown in!' Leaving the soap business in 1893, Hubbard settled in East Aurora near Buffalo, New York, and founded there an ideal 'mediaeval manor' and workers' community, the Roycrofters.

In 1894 he visited England, met William Morris, and fell under the spell of the Kelmscott Press. Back home he began to publish a magazine, *The Philistine*, and a long-running series of books, *Little Journeys to the Homes of the Great*, bound in limp chamois bindings. With the salesman's instinct for 'good copy' these journalistic interviews erred towards the sensational, and were perhaps most effectively criticized by Whistler, who wrote a characteristic letter after the publication of a *Little Journey* about him, thanking Hubbard for 'telling me and the world so many interesting things about myself that I never knew before'.

The Roycrofters set up an apprentice system, the workers learning various crafts and attending lectures and concerts on Guild and School of Handicrafts lines, although their activities failed to impress C .R. Ashbee on his visit to East Aurora. They produced adaptions of Stickley's 'Mission' furniture, leather and metal work. But Hubbard's real gifts were as a popularizer. The Roycroft Inn, whose sign still proclaims 'Never Mind. People will talk anyway', became 'the haven of tired businessmen, the rendezvous of honeymooners', and the leather and gift shop became major tourist attractions. These activities brought a sincere, if over-simplified, version of Arts and Crafts ideals to a very wide public. By 1905, a separate furniture catalogue was issued, which proclaimed proudly, 'A room furnished Roycroftie is a constant delight to the owner and occupant'.

Roycroft sentiments, and a liberal infusion of the ideas of Thoreau, to whom the book is dedicated, are reflected in a popular novel of the period, Gene Stratton Porter's *The Harvester*. The hero, a handsome herbalist, whose hobby is carving wooden candlesticks decorated with moths, builds a log cabin for the heroine, which is decorated in a very 'Roycroftie' mission style:

He led her into what had been the front room of the old cabin, now a large, long dining room having on each side wide windows with deep seats ... All the woodwork, chairs, the dining table, cupboards, and carving table were golden oak. Only a few rugs and furnishings and a woman's touch were required to make it an unusual and beautiful room. The kitchen was shining with a white hard-wood floor, white wood-work, and pale green walls ... [Upstairs], the Girl stood and looked around her with amazed eyes. The floor was pale yellow wood, polished until it shone like a table top. The casings, table, chairs, dressing table,

180, 181 Pages from the Roycroft catalogue, 1910, showing the diversity of objects designed by Elbert Hubbard's company

TITLE-PAGE FROM "THE MINTAGE"
By Dard Hunter

180

THE MINTAGE

BEING A BOOK OF TEN STORIES, AND ONE MORE

By Elbert Hubbard

¶ The Short Story is the most exacting form of literature that can be produced. It is like high-class Vaudeville—it must grip the hearts and minds of every one, and do it from the very first utterance. One word too much, or one too little, and you have lost your auditor. The short story is the diamond of letters. — *Anatole France.*

¶ Frank Putnam has called Elbert Hubbard the Anatole France of America, "on account of his liquid language and flawless style."

¶ Everybody who even peeps into books admits that Elbert Hubbard has the concentration which constitutes literary style; some think he has genius; a few believe that as a writer (not to mention thinker and doer) he has no living equal.

¶ A woman who belongs to this last class has selected these stories and called them "The Mintage" because they are. They scintillate with wit, dazzle with insight, seize with emotion, lure with their love and sympathy.

¶ Great literature is born of feeling. There is only one kind of ink—and that is red. The man or woman who can read "The Mintage" without tears has left his heyday behind the hill and is heading for the Silence.

¶ "The Mintage" is on Italian handmade paper, bound "Miriam"—solid boards, designed leather backs, quite artcrafty and some bosarty—Two Dollars a copy, carriage prepaid.

[15]

HAND-CARVED MOTTOS

¶ These mottos are made on half-logs and boards. The half-logs are hung from hand-wrought chains, and some of the boards are mounted with copper bands.

¶ Such mottos are especially attractive in the reception-hall or over the fireplace, where they express your greeting to the stranger or a welcome to your friend.

¶ We make them to any measurement—and carve your motto. Special mottos, of course, take time. The human hand is a very delicate machine and does not turn out its product at a breathless speed.

¶ Three weeks from the time a special order is received we will be able to ship to you.

¶ Is three weeks too long to wait? Fra Elbertus has a few good mottos of his own. Some say this adds a value—judge for yourself, here is our list.

MADE ON HALF-LOGS

10 INCHES X 42 INCHES

1	Be yourself	$4.50
2	Build strong	4.75

181 [126]

ROYCROFT LEATHER BALLS

L-113, Medicine-Ball, weight 5 lbs. $5.00

   Hand-Balls
Also used for indoor baseball

L-115, $1.00   L-117, $ .50

L-119, Medicine-Ball, weight 3 lbs. $3.00

[88]

155

182 Oak chair from the Roycroft shops, East Aurora, New York (Art Museum, Princeton University)

chest of drawers, and bed were solid curly maple. The doors were big polished slabs of it, each containing enough material to veneer all the furniture in the room. The walls were of plaster, tinted yellow, and the windows with yellow shades were curtained in dainty white ... She stepped on deep rugs of yellow goat skins ...

'What planning! What work!' she sobbed. 'What taste! Why he's a poet!'

Hubbard, and his wife Alice, died tragically, when the liner the 'Lusitania' was sunk in 1915. The apocryphal story that after the German torpedo struck, Hubbard remarked to his wife, 'Think of it

Alice—tomorrow the headlines will say "Elbert Hubbard killed on the Lusitania",' cannot be verified, but is in keeping with his character, and certainly his dramatic death added to the charisma of his legend, bringing a posthumous fame that helped to keep the Roycroft institution going as a business until 1938.

Stickley and Hubbard's names are today virtually forgotten outside specialized collecting and academic circles. The name of Louis Comfort Tiffany (1848–1933) remains widely known, with the glamour befitting a great jeweller and producer of the most opulent of all Art Nouveau artifacts, the pendant 'Tiffany' lamps and irridescent glass which are so associated with his name. Yet the pattern of his life also reflects his admiration of the craft ideals of William Morris. His interior decoration studio, 'Louis C. Tiffany, Associated Artists', established in New York in 1879, was set up in emulation of Morris and Company. But glass, his obsessive passion, is, by its very viscosity, the ideal Art Nouveau medium, and Tiffany's great achievements do not therefore fall within the scope of this book.

Another figure with affiliations in both camps was the Art Nouveau poster designer, Will H. Bradley (1868–1962). His posters and book illustrations have remained better known than his decorative art work, published in *The Ladies Home Journal* between 1901 and 1905. His house interiors, while they reflect the ideas of Voysey, and even more Baillie Scott, have a distinctive cohesiveness which is all his own.

The most rewarding merger of Art Nouveau and Arts and Crafts styles is perhaps provided in the work of Charles Rohlfs (1853–1936), who started life as a designer of cast iron stoves before turning to the stage and becoming a well known Shakespearean actor. He became a furniture designer after marriage to a novelist, who married him on condition that he gave up acting. He produced a number of pieces which were hailed with enthusiasm at the Buffalo exhibition of 1901, Turin in 1902, and St. Louis in 1904. The chest of drawers shown here (in Fig. 183), intended for use in his own home, is a simplified version of one shown with great success at those exhibitions. Rohlf's son remembers his father explaining that the carved design on the side was inspired by the smoke curling from his pipe as he worked.

California and the Pacific coast also provide some notable excursions into Arts and Crafts territory. The Arroyo Guild of Los Angeles adapted Stickley's motto *Als ik Kan* to the perhaps over confident 'We Can'! But nowhere in the United States was the movement to play a more important role than in the mid-west and Chicago, culminating in what is now known as the Prairie School of architecture and the early work of Frank Lloyd Wright (1869–1959).

The founder of the Prairie School was the revolutionary architect Louis H. Sullivan (1856–1924). His architectural importance has been frequently discussed, and needs no reiteration here, except in so far as his theories of decoration, elaborated in his book *Ornament in Architecture*, of 1892, were to influence Wright. In it, despite his own

183 Charles Rohlfs chest of
drawers in fumed oak, 1900
(Art Museum, Princeton
University)

184 Detail from Charles
Rohlfs chest of drawers

unique ability to animate the austere blocks of his major Chicago buildings with luxuriant Art Nouveau decoration, Sullivan advocates that 'ornament is mentally a luxury, not a necessary', and that 'it would be greatly for our aesthetic good, if we should refrain from the use of ornament for a period of years.'

During his five years in Sullivan's office as chief draughtsman from 1888–1893, Wright fully absorbed these teachings. His own early work as interior designer was to show a rare ability to treat furniture, not as providing areas for ornamental embellishment, but with a sculptor's feeling for simple mass and form. The close relationship of the exterior of his buildings with their uncluttered interiors, with much of the furniture built into the walls, reflected what became a life-long admiration of Japanese architecture.

A classic demonstration of these qualities in one interior is provided by the dining room furniture designed for the Frederick C. Robie house in Chicago, illustrated in Fig. 185. The vertical elements provided by the chairbacks and four piers with lamps produce an enclosed, protective space around the dining table at which the family gathered, a dramatic creation worthy of Appia or Gordon Craig.

But these early works also show an affinity with Arts and Crafts ideas. This is hardly surprising, for in the 1880s and 1890s Chicago society took a keen interest in the works of William Morris. This was largely due to the frequent lectures of Joseph Twyman (1842–1904), an Englishman who had settled in the city and established a Morris showroom at the Toby Furniture Company, where chintzes and wallpapers could be readily obtained. English celebrities also helped to popularize the movement. Oscar Wilde, in 1882, spoke on 'House Decoration', 'Decorative Art in America' and 'The English Renaissance', and wrote home triumphantly about his huge fee of $1000—£200 for one hour. In 1891, Walter Crane lectured on 'Art and Modern Life' and 'Design in Relation to Use and Materials'.

But the most notable English visitor to Chicago was C. R. Ashbee, who made three visits in 1896, 1901, and 1908, and found the city most congenial. In 1901, he wrote, after visiting fourteen American states, 'Chicago is the only American city I have seen where something absolutely distinctive in aesthetic handling of materials has been evolved out of the industrial system'. This visit was made on a fund-raising tour on behalf of the National Trust, and while in Chicago Ashbee delivered ten lectures before appreciative audiences. One long-term result of this stay was to be the friendship which developed between Ashbee and Wright, who volunteered to serve as the local secretary of the National Trust. The friendship, which was to last throughout their lives,* was based on the attraction of opposites, for both men held strong and opposed views on the arts, and enjoyed vigorous arguments over design theories.

After one discussion in 1901, Ashbee noted in his journal:

Wright threw down the glove to me in characteristic Chicagoan manner when

159

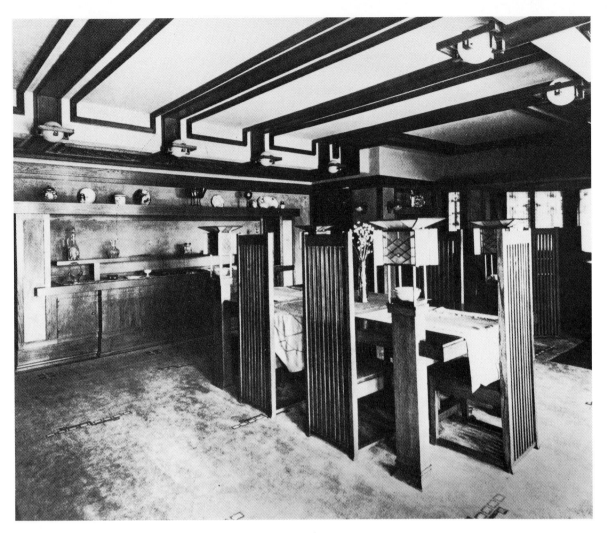

185 Frank Lloyd Wright, the
Robie House, Chicago
(Mr and Mrs Robert L.
Jacobson)

we discussed the Arts and Crafts. 'My God', he said, 'is machinery, and the art of
the future will be the expression of the individual artist through the thousand
powers of the machine—the machine doing all those things that the individual
workman cannot do. The creative artist is the man who controls all this and
understands it'.

These ideas were to be fully developed in Wright's important lecture
later that year on 'The Art and Craft of the Machine'. The lecture was
delivered at Hull House, the home of the Chicago Arts and Crafts
Society founded in 1897. It will always rank as one of the key statements
of intent in twentieth-century art and design, and demands extensive
quotation here, since the passionate sincerity of Wright's arguments
still remain of the utmost relevance in any discussion of the role of
craftsmanship in contemporary society.

Wright begins with an impassioned plea to architects and modern
society to come to terms with the machine and the new and exciting
opportunities which it gives to design in fresh ways. He regrets the way

in which art students are 'taught in the name of John Ruskin or William Morris to shun and despise the essential tool of their age as a matter commercial and antagonistic to art'.

But his greatest scorn is reserved for the field in which he had already made so many significant innovations—the design of the house. He castigates 'the theatrical desire on the part of fairly respectable people to live in Chateaux, Manor Houses, Venetian Palaces, Feudal Castles, and Queen Anne Cottages:

Look within all this typical monotony-in-variety and see there the machine-made copies of handicraft originals; in fact, unless you, the householder, are fortunate indeed, possessed of extraordinary taste and opportunity, all you possess is in some degree a machine-made example of vitiated handicraft, imitation antique furniture made antique by the machine, itself of all abominations the most abominable . . . Here we have the curse of stupidity—a cheap substitute for ancient art and craft which has no vital meaning in your own life or our time.

He then discusses the perversion of the machine into these ignoble uses:

Let us now glance at wood. Elaborate machinery has been invented for no other purpose than to imitate the wood-carving of early handicraft patterns. Result? No good joinery. None saleable without some horrible glued-on botch-work meaning nothing, unless it means that 'Art and Craft' (by salesmanship) has fixed in the minds of the masses the elaborate hand-carved chair as ultimate ideal . . . The beauty of wood lies in its qualities as wood, strange as this may seem. Why does it take so much imagination just to see that? Treatments that fail to bring out those qualities, foremost, are not *plastic*, therefore no longer appropriate . . .

The Machines used in woodwork will show that by unlimited power in cutting, shaping, smoothing, and by the tireless repeat, they have emancipated beauties of wood nature, making possible without waste, beautiful surface treatments and clean strong forms that veneers of Sheraton or Hepplewhite only hinted at with dire extravagance . . . But the advantages of the machines are wasted and we suffer from a riot of aesthetic murder and everywhere live with debased handicraft.

The coda of the lecture urges the rightful use of the machine to liberate the arts:

. . . the artist is now free to work his rational will with freedoms unknown to structural tradition. Units of construction have enlarged, rhythms have been simplified and etherealized, space is more spacious and the sense of it may enter into every building, great or small. Rightly used the very curse machinery puts upon handicraft should emancipate the artist from the temptation to petty structural deceit and end this wearisome struggle to make things seem what they are not and can never be.

He concludes in stirring words:

The day of the individual is not over-instead it is just about to begin. The Machine does not write the doom of Liberty, but is waiting at man's hand as a peerless tool, . . . What limits do we dare imagine to an art that is organic fruit of an adequate life for the individual! Although this power is now murderous, chained to botch work and bungler's ambitions, the creative Artist will surely take it into his hand, and, in the name of Liberty, swiftly undo the deadly mischief it has created.

The Arts and Crafts movement, in both America and England, was never to be the same again, for his words mark the beginning of the rejection of Ruskin and Morris's advocacy of hand craftsmanship as the only solution to social, architectural and artistic problems.

In 1905 Wright was to visit Japan, and there absorbed his life-long respect for the subtle forms of Japanese architecture. His departure for Europe in 1909 marks the end of his first great phase as an architect and of his involvement with Arts and Crafts theories.

The end of the Arts and Crafts movement in America, like its end in England and Europe, can be dated at 1916, the year which saw in New York City the opening of the Armoury Show, the major landmark in the beginnings of modern art, with its important abstract works by Brancusi and Arp, and the appearance of the final issue of *The Craftsman* magazine. These two events aptly symbolize the passing of the old order and the beginning of the new. A year later, America entered the first world war. The doughboy's song:

'How are they going to keep 'em,
Down on the Farm,
Now that they've seen Paree?'

was also, ironically, the swansong of the Arts and Crafts movement in America. On their return to their 'Main Streets' in the Gopher Prairies of the American mid-west, the Babbits of the post-war years shook off the 'out of date' styles of the Arts and Crafts movement and the Prairie School, only to embrace the Tudor and Colonial period houses. The age of the Ford car, the Wall Street collapse and the Depression beset America. When the regeneration of American architecture took place, it looked to Europe again for inspiration, to the work of such key modern architects as Mies Van der Rohe. But for the arts the break with the past symbolized by the Armoury show led to quite different departures which culminated in the establishment of the abstract expressionist school, a powerfully indigenous form owing nothing to European sources.

In the thirty years of its existence the Arts and Crafts movement in America evolved from a provincial and imitative echoing of British prototypes to produce in Wright, Tiffany and Stickley figures of central significance in the movement's history.

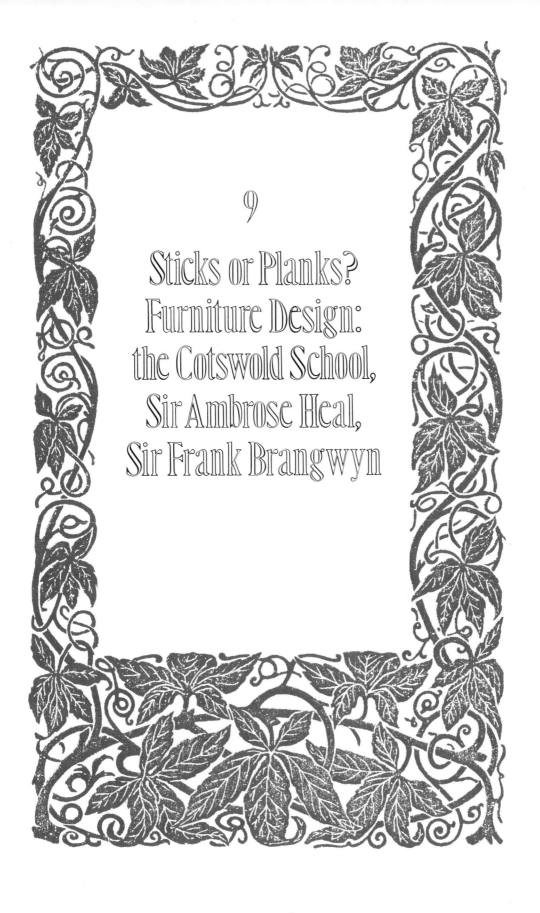

9

Sticks or Planks?
Furniture Design:
the Cotswold School,
Sir Ambrose Heal,
Sir Frank Brangwyn

ILLIAM MORRIS gave a lecture early in 1844 in the Secular Hall, Leicester. Among the audience was the twenty year old Ernest Gimson, who afterwards asked Morris for advice on his future career. Morris recommended him to study craft traditions and article himself to the aesthetic architect John Dando Sedding, whose Holy Trinity Church, Sloane Street is one of the finest Arts and Crafts buildings. Rarely can advice have had such far-reaching results.

Sedding's London offices were next door to Morris and Company's main showrooms, and Grimson was thus placed in daily visual contact with wallpapers and chintzes which greatly appealed to his innate sense of pattern making. W. R. Lethaby records Gimson's early practice of taking a large piece of Morris chintz with him on holiday as an easy way of 'having something to look at'. This love of patterns was to find expression in the devoted attention with which Gimson studied the art of the plasterer while articled to Sedding. He studied old plasterwork at Speke Hall, Chastleton and Orpington, and acquired practical knowledge of the craft, the only one in which he ever attained great technical proficiency, by working at Messrs. Whitcombe and Prestly, the leading workers of those days. But Gimson's own imaginative patterns were to hark back to an age of design far more vigorous than the degenerate florid revampings of baroque and rococo themes then in fashion.

In *The Dream of John Ball* Morris had imagined a Rose Tavern in Richard II's day:

The walls were panelled roughly enough with oak boards to about six feet from the floor and about three feet of plaster above that was wrought in a pattern of a rose stem running all round the room, freely and roughly done, but with (it seemed to my unused eyes) wonderful skill and strength. On the hood of the great chimney a huge rose was wrought in the plaster and brightly painted in its true colours.

In his work at Pinbury and Daneway House Gimson was almost to make this dream a reality. It is tempting to speculate whether this passage of Morris was in his mind when in later years he sketched a design for modelling the end wall of the library of the Cambridge Medical Schools.

During holidays, Gimson also studied the craft of making rush-seated chairs. At a meeting of the Art Workers' Guild shortly after its opening exhibition in 1888 someone produced some chairs by Philip Clissett, a Herefordshire chair bodger from Bosbury. Gimson went to Bosbury and worked with Clissett, and while there he fell under the potent spell of the Cotswolds.

Although these craft studies were important formative influences on his later work, the lifelong friendships which Gimson made at Sedding's were to prove of equal significance in their effect on his career and the formation of the Cotswold School. One of these friendships was with Ernest Barnsley, a fellow student at Sedding's, whose brother Sidney

186 Decorative plasterwork frieze of honeysuckle, oak leaves and squirrels at Pinbury by Ernest Gimson, c. 1893, from a photograph taken in 1911

187 Design for plasterwork, Ernest Gimson, 1903 (Cheltenham Museum and Art Gallery)

164

186

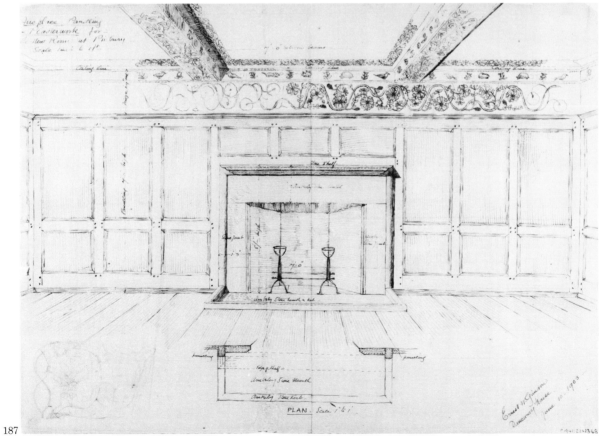

187

188 Philip Clissett, chair
bodger, of Bosbury
(1817–1913). Lithograph by
Maxwell Balfour, published in
The Quarto, 1898

was articled to Norman Shaw. Shaw's chief assistant at this time was
W. R. Lethaby, who was some years older and a friend of Morris and
Philip Webb, from whom he had absorbed the innate feeling for solid
architectural form in the design of furniture which was to become such
a predominant characteristic of the group's activities.

In 1890, Gimson, the two brothers Barnsley, W. R. Lethaby, Mervyn
McCartney and Reginal Blomfield banded together to form Kenton and
Company. This enterprise, significantly named after the street in which
the workshop stood, and not given an idealistic 'Guild' title, was
founded in a similar spirit to that of Morris and Company thirty years
earlier, that is to say relatively lightheartedly, but with the serious
intention of improving design, each member putting up £100 capital.
The major difference between Kenton and Company and its predecessors the Century Guild and the Guild and School of Handicraft was

189 Photograph, 1891, of
Kenton and Company's
exhibition at Barnard's Inn,
showing a chest by Lethaby
and cabinet by Gimson

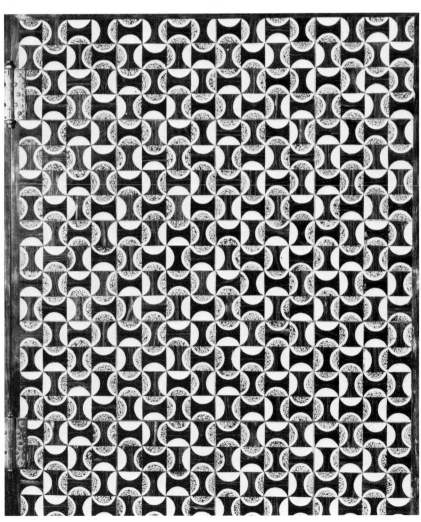

190 Detail of cabinet's door,
inlaid with palm, ebony and
orangewood marquetry (Fine
Art Society)

their relative reticence concerning the social aspects of their self-appointed mission. They issued no manifesto, preferring to direct their energies to experimenting with remarkably daring technical innovations. A contemporary photograph of the Company's exhibition in 1891 shows a chest by W. R. Lethaby decorated with a stylized design of sailing ships and a cabinet by Ernest Gimson, both of which demonstrate the originality of the group's work. The marquetry of the cabinet door designed by Gimson (Fig. 190) is composed of a bold jigsaw of interrelated curves, which cleave together, not by conventional adhesive means, but by the power of longitudinal and vertical stress, producing an effect of exciting natural virtuosity, like a water-boatman skimming across a pool supported only by the surface tension of the water. The real originality of the group's approach to form was also forcibly demonstrated by a work box by W. R. Lethaby, an abstract geometric exercise in volume that is also satisfyingly practical as a design, and astonishingly anticipates the products of the Bauhaus.

Kenton and Company held a successful exhibition at Barnard's Inn in 1891, but came to an end the following year through lack of capital. In 1893, Gimson and the two Barnsley brothers moved to Ewen, near Cirencester, and in 1894 to Pinbury in the aptly named Golden Valley, an idyllic setting for a Utopian craft venture. The woods surrounding the house were alive with squirrels, and Gimson used a squirrel motif to link fire dogs, carving on the chimney breast and plasterwork in a decorative scheme of delightful simplicity. He also built a cottage near the house, and A. H. Powell, another student of Norman Shaw, who settled nearby, becoming a potter and painter, has recorded in his

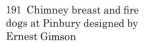
191 Chimney breast and fire dogs at Pinbury designed by Ernest Gimson

191

168

192 Gimson's living room at Pinbury illustrated by A. H. Powell. From *Ernest Gimson* by W. R. Lethaby, 1926

193 Early photograph, *c.* 1900, of the interior of Stoneywell Cottage, Markfield, by Ernest Gimson

192

93

194 Stoneywell Cottage, Markfield, illustrated by F. L. M. Griggs. From *Ernest Gimson* by W. R. Lethaby, 1926

drawing (Fig. 192) of Gimson's living room in the cottage a characteristic feature, the shelf for books running round the room just below the ceiling.

For the next few years Gimson was particularly concerned with architecture, designing several houses of remarkable originality. It is interesting to note in his treatment of the staircase and roof beams (Figs. 195, 196) in the White House, Leicester of 1897, the primitive vigour of the chamfering, creating forms almost comparable with the sculptural power of Yoruba or Dogon tribal art.

The following year, 1898, saw the creation of Gimson's most remarkable early building, Stoneywell Cottage, Markfield, in a remote and rocky part of Charnwood Forest near Leicester. This relatively small building possesses a powerful dramatic quality, as though Philip Webb or Norman Shaw had become excited by a visit to a stage production by Gordon Craig. Its most notable feature is the towering chimney stack which grows out of the rock and leads the eye upwards like the great tower of Ibsen's *Master Builder*. F. L. Grigg's drawing (Fig. 194) gives a vivid impression of this noble structure. Within the building, the subtle articulation of the room interiors provides a

170

constantly stimulating sense of movement and variety. The eye is always being led on to discover new and unexpected angles. The house was built for a cousin of Gimson who also commissioned from Sidney Barnsley a massive dresser and other furniture. During the 1890s Sidney, unlike his brother and Gimson, had concentrated, not on architecture, but on furniture design, evolving many concepts which were to become the basic grammar and syntax of the 'Cotswold School' style. A retiring, austere man of great integrity, he thought it wrong to

195 Roof beams and stairwell, the White House, Leicester, Ernest Gimson

196 Staircase, the White House, Leicester, Ernest Gimson

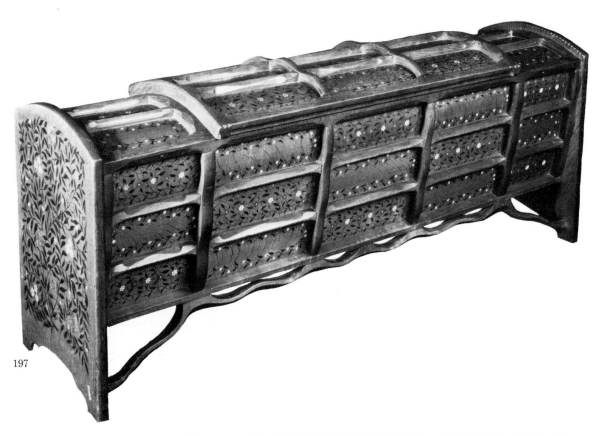

197

197 Oak coffer by Sidney
Barnsley, with painted
decoration by Alfred and
Louise Powell (Fine Art
Society)

198 Sidney Barnsley, portrait
(Craft Study Centre, Bath)

199 Dining table and chairs at
Stoneywell Cottage by Sidney
Barnsley

200 Wedgewood vase
decorated by A. H. Powell in
1909 (Victoria and Albert
Museum)

198

199

200

delegate to others the more routine aspects of cabinet making. He therefore felt unable to join with his brother and Gimson in the partnership they embarked upon in 1900. He wrote to Philip Webb on 6th July, 1902, 'My brother and Gimson have already started workshops at Daneway having four or five cabinet makers and boys so far, with the hope of chairmakers and modellers in the near future. I am remaining an outsider from this movement and still going on making furniture by myself and handing over to them any orders I cannot undertake, and orders seem to come in too quickly now as we are getting known.' Barnsley's work was always notable for its honesty of construction, as is apparent in the restrained simplicity of the massive cabinet illustrated (Fig. 201). The reticence of this piece acts as a foil to his great *tour de force*, the magnificent oak coffer of the mid 1900s (Fig. 197), a great ark of a vessel, ribbed with a rhythmic symmetry that recalls the skeleton of a whale or the vaulted ceiling of a Gothic cathedral. This analogy is perhaps the more fruitful, for just as cathedrals were often gaily painted, so is the coffer delicately ornamented with a design of daisies, scarlet pimpernel and other flowers of the hedgerow executed by Alfred Powell, who often decorated his friends' pieces in this way. His own decorative pottery tended to be far more elaborate in style.

201 Cabinet by Sidney
Barnsley, whereabouts
unknown. This photograph is
produced from an early
negative. Ernest Gimson and
Sidney Barnsley, and later
Peter Waals, employed an
excellent local Cirencester
photographer to make a
complete record of all their
executed pieces.

In 1903 Gimson and the Barnsleys settled permanently at Sapperton in
cottages of their own design. F. L. Griggs's drawing (Fig. 202) of the
north side of Gimson's cottage shows the dormered thatched roof, high
chimney stack, rounded projection for the staircase and the open shed
with the dormer windows of his workroom above, while the drawing of
the south side (Fig. 203) and photograph (Fig. 204) both capture the
quiet tranquility of the house.

Across the valley in the spacious fifteenth-century Daneway House,
Gimson established a workshop employing a number of cabinet makers
under a chief foreman, Peter Van der Waals, a Dutchman from The
Hague, who had learnt his craft in his native Holland and also worked
in Brussels and Berlin. Waals excelled in marquetry work, a virtuoso
example of his talent in this technique being a small box decorated with

202 North side of Gimson's
cottage at Sapperton
illustrated by F. L. M. Griggs,
from *Ernest Gimson*

203 South side of Gimson's cottage at Sapperton, F. L. M. Griggs, from *Ernest Gimson*

204 Early photograph of the south side of Gimson's cottage

a design by Gimson of roses, buds and leaves illustrated (Fig. 205). Such extreme elaboration was exceptional, and in the other examples Gimson preferred to rely on stylized designs carried out with simple inlaying and plain surfaces. These exquisitely made pieces are some of the most attractive products of the Daneway workshop, lacking the high seriousness and portentous gravity which can mar one's appreciation of its larger furniture.

Another craftsman whose work for Gimson was to be of great importance was the blacksmith Alfred Bucknell. Powell first drew Gimson's attention to Bucknell's abilities, and Gimson gave him mediaeval strap hinges (similar to his own designs) and early latches to copy. Bucknell worked at these for some weeks, producing satisfactory

206

205 Box designed by Ernest Gimson, executed by Peter Waals

206 Box designed by Ernest Gimson

207 Box designed by Ernest Gimson (Photographs: Leicester Museum and Art Gallery, whereabouts of boxes unknown, see the note to Fig. 201 on page 174)

207

208 Box designed by Ernest Gimson (Fine Art Society)

209 Designs for hinges and straps by Ernest Gimson, 1905 (Cheltenham Museum and Art Gallery)

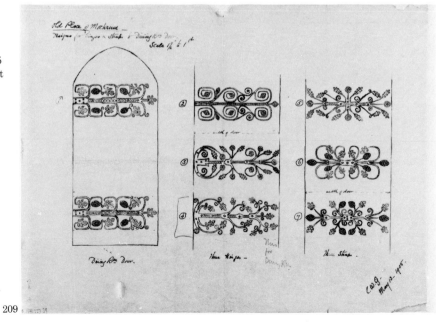

209

178

results, without Gimson making any mention of payment. In desperation Bucknell asked for some wages, whereupon Gimson offered him £1. 1s. 0d. a week. At this Bucknell threatened to leave immediately as he was getting £1. 5s. 0d. a week at his old job. This wage dispute must have been settled amicably, for Bucknell remained with Gimson for many years. Among the work which he produced to Gimson's designs, pride of place must be afforded to the handsome fire dogs, which were greatly in demand for the large fireplaces of local Cotswold houses. Gimson had studied sixteenth-century examples at Haddon Hall and elsewhere, but evolved his own variations on the traditional forms. Wall sconces were another favourite theme providing scope for Gimson's stylized treatment of such natural forms as acorns, oak leaves, flowers and foliage. Domestic and ecclesiastical candelabra and crosses, candlesticks, fire irons, and toasting forks were produced, and Bucknell also made the handles and fittings for the furniture produced at Daneway. After Gimson's death Bucknell continued to work for Peter Van der Waals at Chalford, and his son Norman Bucknell continues to produce fine metalwork today.

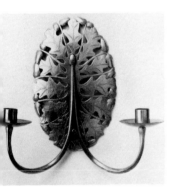

210 Sconce, designed by Gimson and executed by Alfred Bucknell (Fine Art Society)

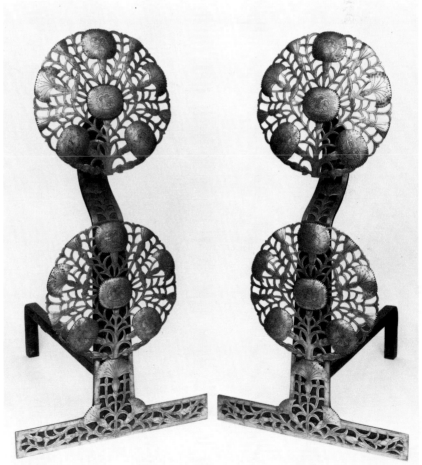

211 Firedogs in steel designed by Ernest Gimson, c. 1905. Executed by Alfred Bucknell (Fine Art Society)

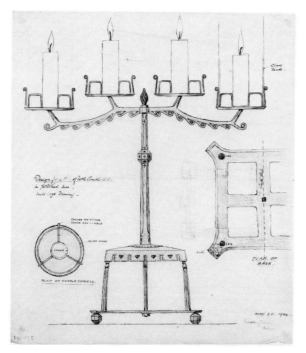

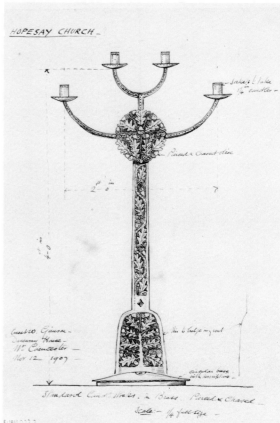

213

212 Design for table candlestick by Gimson, 1904 (Cheltenham Museum and Art Gallery)

213 Design for candlestick for Hopesay Church by Gimson, 1907 (Cheltenham Museum and Art Gallery)

214 Altar cross and candlestick, St. Andrew's, Roker, Sunderland, in polished wrought iron, designed by Gimson and executed by Alfred Bucknell, 1906–7

214

Contact with architectural colleagues in London resulted in a number of important ecclesiatical commissions for Gimson, notably St. Andrew's, Roker, Sunderland, by E. S. Prior, and the St. Andrew's Chapel in Westminster Cathedral. A representative example of this work is the altar cross in ebony and ivory, inlaid with red coral set in silver, presented in memory of Keith Debenham to the Church of St. Peter, Vere Street, London, by Charles Debenham, one of Gimson's most important London patrons. For Debenham's famous shop, Gimson executed one of his finest plasterwork schemes, now unfortunately boarded over, in the third floor restaurant, although some splendid ceilings can still be seen in the ladies' lingerie department.

Yet the most important and well-known aspect of the work of the Daneway workshop was its production of furniture. Like the Lord High Admiral in Gilbert and Sullivan's *H.M.S. Pinafore*, Gimson, 'never,— well hardly ever' actually made furniture himself, apart from rush-seated chairs, and simple pieces for his own use. But he possessed a profound knowledge of the problems involved in cabinet making, and a

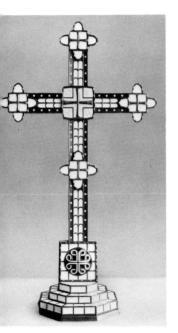

215 Altar cross, St. Peter's, Vere Street, London, designed by Ernest Gimson

216 Fire-irons and toasting fork designed by Gimson and executed by Alfred Bucknell

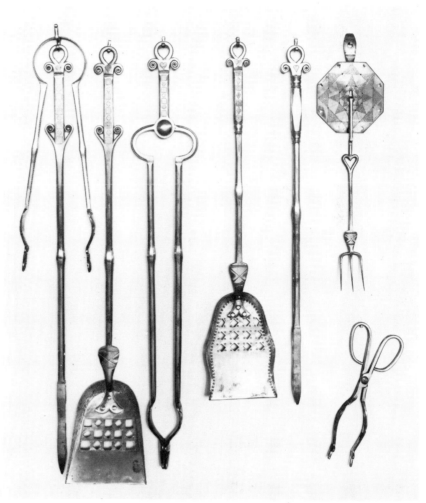

216

181

rare willingness to allow his designs to be modified after discussion with the individual craftsman doing the job. When, for example, Harry Davoll, entrusted with the making of a segmental sideboard in English oak, queried the unnecessary heaviness of the centre posts, Gimson, after a little thought, agreed, and the piece was amended accordingly. This respect for the interpretative abilities of the executant is one of the main points of resemblance between Morris and Gimson, and indeed the productions of the Daneway workshops seem to exemplify the criteria demanded by William Morris in his lecture, 'The Lesser Arts of Life':

So I say our furniture should be good citizen's furniture, solid and well made in workmanship, and in design should have nothing about it that is not easily defensible, no monstrosities or extravagances, not even of beauty, lest we weary of it . . . also I think that, except for very movable things like chairs it should not be so very light as to be nearly imponderable; it should be made of timber rather than walking sticks . . . Moreover I must need think of furniture as of two kinds: one part of it being chairs, dining and working tables, and the like, the

217 Bobbin-turned rush-seated settle, designed by Gimson, made by Edward Gardiner (photograph from an original negative: see the note to Fig. 201 on page 174)

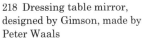

218 Dressing table mirror, designed by Gimson, made by Peter Waals

219 Cabined designed by Gimson (see the note to Fig. 201 on page 174)

necessary work-a-day furniture in short, which should be of course well made and well proportioned, but simple to the last degree; nay, if it were rough I should like it better . . . but besides this kind of furniture, there is what I should call state furniture, which I think is quite proper even for a citizen; I mean sideboards, cabinets and the like, which we have quite as much for beauty's sake as for use; we need not spare ornament on these, but may make them as elegant and elaborate as we can with carving, inlaying, or painting, these are the blossoms of the art of furniture.

Gimson's cabinets, and such basic pieces as the looking glass, exactly fulfill these requirements, but it is at the same time possible to agree with the anonymous critic of *The Builder* who in 1916, reviewing the Arts and Crafts Exhibition, wrote of Gimson's furniture, 'his theory of design is lamentable. The fault inheres in narrowness of outlook, in a blind attempt to build up a new system of design for movables based on the requirements of the peasant, and in a vain attempt to stretch rude simplicity into terms of rich and pompous complexity. Such methods

220 Cabinet designed by
Gimson in the early 1900s
(whereabouts unknown:
photographs from a
contemporary negative)

221 The same cabinet
with doors open

might, and probably do, ensnare the uninitiated, but the educated man rebels at the idea of being treated as a glorified peasant . . .'

These qualities, which might facetiously be called 'the self importance of being Earnest', are perhaps most evident in the device of chamfered supports to tables (see below). These tables illustrate the initial basic and satisfying adaptation by Gimson of the cruck of a Gloucestershire farm waggon to the stretchers of a dining table; but this happy device becomes in the second example shown (Fig. 223) merely a self-conscious mannerism, rather than a natural deviation from a craft source.

Shortly before his death in 1919 at the relatively early age of 54, Gimson designed the Memorial Library and other buildings at Bedales

222, 223 Two Gimson tables with chamfered stretchers (photographs from the original negatives: see note to Fig. 201)

222

223

185

224 Drop-front chest by Peter Waals (photograph from an original negative: see note to Fig. 201)

School, near Petersfield in Hampshire. The Library possesses obvious similarities with William Morris's beloved tithe barn at Great Coxwell, Gloucestershire. His thoughts at this time also turned, in a letter to Sidney Cockerell, to a characteristic Utopian theme, the foundation of a craftsman village for demobilized soldiers after the World War, a dream to remain unrealized.

After Gimson's death, Ernest and Sidney Barnsley were to realize in the building of Rodmarton Manor one of the most impressive of the Cotswold enterprises, the creation of one of the last great houses built in England. Gimson's foreman Peter Van der Waals continued to produce furniture in workshops in Chalford a few miles away. His productions continued the simplicity of Gimson's design principles, but his love of marquetry work sometimes resulted in over-elaboration. Yet Waals was an original designer in his own right. Of a similar wardrobe to the one illustrated (Fig. 225) he wrote, 'I made this as a protest against the dull flat surfaces in modern furniture. Mass made furniture could be enlivened by the play of light on the simple fielding of small panels'.

225 Wardrobe by Peter Waals (photograph from an original negative: see note to Fig. 201)

The contribution of Gimson, the Barnsleys and Waals to the Arts and Crafts movement was a major one, which still remains relatively unacknowledged and little known. In his lecture on 'Art and Industry', William Morris said, 'I do not mean that . . . we should aim at abolishing all machinery: I would do some things by machinery that are now done by hand, and other things by hand that are now done by machinery: in short, we should be the masters of our machines, and not their slaves as we are now'. Gimson, who in so many respects resembles Morris, shared this view, and it is too simplistic to summarize his contribution to the Arts and Crafts movement as a purely historicist one of a return to earlier craft methods. Like Morris he did not totally condemn the machine, and once prophetically remarked, 'Let machinery be honest and make its own machine buildings and its own machine furniture; let it make its chairs of stamped aluminium if it likes: why not?'

While Gimson's work was to have a continuing influence on English furniture design throughout the first half of this century, mention should be made here of the most notable of his contemporaries.

226 *Weavers and Spinners* mural by Brangwyn (Leeds Art Gallery)

227 Wardrobe by Ambrose Heal in oak inlaid with pewter and ebony made by Heal and Sons, 1900. Heals' early pieces have an endearing sparkle

Sir Ambrose Heal (1872–1959) was educated at Marlborough and the Slade school, before serving an apprenticeship as a cabinet maker from 1890 to 1893. In 1896 he began to design furniture for his family's long established firm of Heal and Sons, which faithfully reflected Arts and Crafts principles, yet produced successful and efficiently marketed commercial productions. Ebony, pearwood, and mother-of-pearl were used with great flair and sparkle to enliven plain surfaces of ash, oak and mahogany, the latter a wood eschewed by Gimson and his school. A delightful little pamphlet entitled *Workmanship*, embellished with woodcuts, gives Heal's views on machine production:

In the production of the best modern furniture the machine is sedulously kept in its proper place. The sawing of planks from the rough and the rough planing or smoothing of them are evidently operations which admit of no magic quality being imparted to them by the hand of the workman. The machine just happens to be speedier, relieves the workman of a good deal of drudgery, and legitimately cheapens production.

228 Brangwyn dresser with abstract marquetry pattern (William Morris Gallery)

For **Sir Frank Brangwyn** (1867–1956), designing furniture was only one of many interests, for he was a quintessential artist craftsman, whose career overlaps with many key figures of the period. Born in Bruges, but educated in England, Brangwyn was discovered by A. H. Mackmurdo drawing plaster casts of Italian sculpture at South Kensington, and he introduced him to William Morris for whom he worked from 1882 to 1884 designing tapestry cartoons. After a picaresque interlude serving as a sailor 'before the mast', from 1895 to 1896 Brangwyn worked for S. Bing's 'L'Art Nouveau' in Paris, designing carpets, rugs, textiles, tapestries and stained glass. In 1900, for Bing's stand at the Paris Exhibition, Brangwyn produced his first complete interior decorative scheme with furniture. He later worked for Tiffany of New York. During this period he also designed jewellery and metalwork and for a Leeds manufacturer, a powerful mural of industrial labour (see Fig. 226).

Brangwyn's early furniture was influenced by Heywood Sumner and other Arts and Crafts exponents of *gesso* decoration. A cherrywood cabinet of 1910, made by Paul Turpin, is decorated with carved and coloured *gesso* showing mediaeval figures confronting a flamingo in a fantastic setting. A dresser of a few years later is remarkable for its Art Deco marquetry decoration.

229 Brangwyn's ceramic service for Doulton, displayed in a dresser also designed by Brangwyn (William Morris Gallery)

230 Jug designed by
Brangwyn for Royal Doulton,
late 1920s (author's collection)

In 1926 he designed pottery for Doulton and Co., marked 'Brangwyn-ware', like the jug illustrated here with incised and painted decoration of grapes and vines. These wares proved popular and were followed by a dinner service in dark green and yellow glazes with under-glaze decoration, made in Burslem in 1930.

All these activities would be achievement enough, but were in fact only incidental to his main career as a mural painter and etcher. In 1908 he had a remarkable pupil, Bernard Leach, who studied engraving techniques with him. Brangwyn's career thus links Mackmurdo, Morris and Leach, and provides in its very diversity a microcosm of the whole range of activities of the Arts and Crafts movement.

10

The Unexpected
Legacy

HOMAS HARDY'S NOVEL *Under the Greenwood Tree*, written in 1872, has for its theme the acquisition by an early Victorian vicar of a new church organ, and his attempts to dissolve the traditional village choir. In this, his first successful novel, Hardy's life-long concern for the decline of the old close-knit rural community life found a brilliant comic expression. His later novels and poetry were to return to other aspects of this process, and form the most moving statements of the deepening sense of loss that preoccupied intellectual activities at this time. This sense of deprivation showed itself in a concern that the pleasures and customs of the old order of rural England should be recorded and preserved before they became swamped by technological and commercial interests and the growth of the new urban and suburban England.

The work of the musicologist Cecil Sharp (1859–1924) in the English Folk Song and Dance Societies was to be of major significance in this field. As the foundation stone of Cecil Sharp House records, 'This building is erected in memory of Cecil Sharp who restored to the English people the songs and dances of their country'. His work and teachings,

231 Portrait of Cecil Sharp by William Rothenstein (Cecil Sharp House)

232 Percy Grainger by Maxwell Armfield (Fine Art Society)

194

which remain today a living force, were to inspire figures as various as the composers Frederick Delius, Percy Grainger and Ralph Vaughan Williams; while C. R. Ashbee at Chipping Campden, and Mrs. Gimson at Sapperton both became keen enthusiasts for folk songs and country dancing.

In a closely related field Arnold Dolmetsch (1858–1940) achieved a revival that continues to have a lasting effect on both music and the craft of instrument making. In a fascinating account of the beginning of his career, he writes:

233 Portrait of Arnold Dolmetsch, the founder of the Dolmetsch Workshops

In 1889 in the British Museum, I found an immense collection of English instrumental music of the sixteenth and seventeenth centuries. I resolved to play these pieces which had so fascinated me. Fortunately I felt from the first that this music would only be effective if played upon the instruments for which it was written.

Viols, Lutes, Virginals and Clavichords had not yet become the prey of collectors. I had no great difficulty in procuring some. Having failed to find anybody who could put these instruments in sufficiently good playing order to satisfy my requirements, I remembered that I was a craftsman. I soon rigged up a workshop in the attic of my house and began to work. . . .

William Morris was much interested by our performances. He had for long deplored the fact that, amongst all the Arts, Music alone had no attraction for him. He could find no pleasure in piano recitals and big orchestras; but, when he heard the kind of music whose ideals and purposes correspond with the arts he

234, 235 The harpsichord
made by Arnold Dolmetsch in
1896. The decoration is
painted by Mrs Roger Fry,
roman lettering painted by
Herbert Horne, medieval
notation and inscription
painted by Selwyn Image (Carl
Dolmetsch)

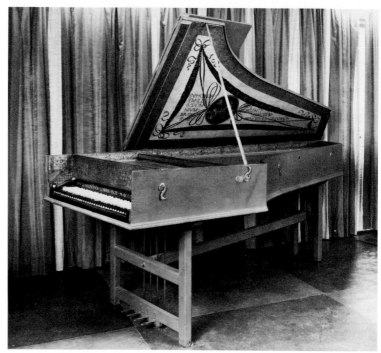

loved, he was profoundly moved. He was ever grateful to me for having filled in his all-embracing mind the place that music alone could fill. Amongst other great men who appreciated my early efforts and encouraged me to persevere, I remember Herbert Horne, Burne-Jones, Selwyn Image . . . and others.

The dawn of a great revival was now visible; but I realized that no serious progress could be made with the scanty stock of old instruments available.

In 1894 I began making clavichords, copies of a fine large instrument in my possession. These instruments succeeded well, but I understood that copying other people's work, the best training for a beginner, should only be a step for higher achievements. The masters did not copy one another. Feeling that I had imagination and skill, I endeavoured henceforth to realize my own ideals.

In 1896 I planned a harpsichord on new lines. It was intended to play the thoroughbass in Bach's *St. Matthew Passion* and to accompany the recitatives of Mozart's operas at Covent Garden. Selwyn Image composed an eloquent Latin inscription which Herbert Horne painted in beautiful letters on the lid. Helen Coombe [afterwards Mrs. Roger Fry] decorated the inside with exquisite flowers and figures. We had planned to ornament the outside also, but, time pressing it was lacquered a fine green.

William Morris, then sickening for death, took a lively interest in this harpsichord and *would* be informed of my plans and progress. His hope of seeing it finished was, alas, frustrated. Feeling the end approaching, he sent for me and a Virginals, desiring to hear once more the old English tunes he loved so well. He died before the opening of the Arts and Crafts Exhibition of 1896. My harpsichord was well received there, but, how I wished Morris had seen it! How I missed the appreciation and criticisms of this great master and inspirer!

Dolmetsch was later to formulate his principles in a credo with obvious parallels with Arts and Crafts theories: 'This music is of absolute and not antiquarian importance; it must be played as the composer intended and on the instruments for which it was written with their correct technique; and through it personal music-making can be restored to the home, from which two centuries of professionalism have divorced it'. These theories were put into practice by the manufacture of such long vanished instruments as the harpsichord, viol, and particularly the recorder, which started a musical revolution the effects of which are still felt today in the activities of musicians like his son, Carl Dolmetsch, the late David Munrow, and craftsmen like Stephen Gottlieb, whose lutes are superlative demonstrations of the continuing and inevitable validity of hand-made musical instruments. In Dolmetsch's words, 'A musical instrument that is to produce beautiful sounds will inevitably be beautiful in appearance.'

The theatre, like music, had close associations with the ideology of the Arts and Crafts movement. The greatest innovatory genius of twentieth-century British theatrical design, Edward Gordon Craig (1872–1966) began his career with the publication of such works as *The Portfolio* and *Penny Toys*, illustrated with woodcuts implicit with the simplicity of early Arts and Crafts design, before developing his later

PHŒBUS.

I am a Penny Pony,
Very like the Troy one,
Made of Wood,
Misunderstood,
Buy your little boy one.

236 Gordon Craig's *Penny Toys*

revolutionary theatrical ideas. Figures like Lilian Baylis and Sir Barry Jackson were motivated by concerns not dissimilar from their Arts and Crafts contemporaries. They founded the repertory system which keeps alive the art of the theatre where commercial managements have succumbed to the successive competition of the cinema and television. In the related field of puppetry, the neglected Cotswold figure of William Simmonds (1876–1968) the sculptor should also be mentioned. He played a leading part in the foundation of the Guild of Puppeteers, in 1900, which brought fresh vitality to one of the oldest art forms, an institution which still flourishes vigorously today.

Old buildings, like old music and dances, also aroused conservationist consciences among members of the Arts and Crafts movement. The threat of over-zealous 'restoration', led William Morris to found the Society for the Preservation of Ancient Buildings in 1877, a group whose activities were promoted by W. R. Lethaby, Philip Webb, Ernest Gimson and other leading figures. In 1894, the National Trust was founded, its aims being to preserve both buildings of artistic and historic interest and threatened areas of the English countryside, one of the moving spirits of the scheme being Canon Rawnsley, founder of the Keswick School of Industrial Art. In 1896, the Clergy House at Alfriston in Sussex became, for £10, the first building to be purchased by the National Trust—a structure with obvious appeal to such vigorous

237 William Simmonds, sleeping calf carved in stone (Fine Art Society). A fine retrospective exhibition of Simmonds's work was assembled at Cheltenham Art Gallery in 1980, but his work is regrettably still little known outside the Cotswolds

238 Stephen Gottlieb, small arch lute

adherents to the Trust's aims as C. R. Ashbee, who became one of their chief early fund raisers, both in this country and by giving lecture tours in America.

The foundation of these societies and activities, which happily continue to flourish, are unexpectedly in some respects the most important legacy of the Arts and Crafts movement to posterity. The shift in emphasis of the main aims of the movement, and its achievements after the watershed of the first world war, are far more difficult to evaluate.

239 Alfriston, Sussex, the first National Trust property, acquired in 1896 (National Trust)

11
Phoenix
or
Chameleon?

HE 1916 EXHIBITION of the Arts and Crafts Exhibition Society can in many ways be described as the swansong of the movement. The battle for parity with the arts, for so long the main aim of the Society, had been won, and the citadel of the Royal Academy successfully stormed, but the victory had proved a hollow one. The more far-sighted members of the group realized that in the postwar years their problems would be very different ones. They foresaw that the nettle of collaboration with industry would have to be firmly grasped. In a paper on Arts, Crafts and Industry, Henry Wilson, the President of the Society, said:

None of the three could properly exist or reach its full development without the others—each must be in harmonious relations with the other two ... The fundamental defect of machine work had been that the expenditure of thought on the product had not been equal to that displayed in the making of the machine. Wages had been cut down to the lowest possible limit, whereas to get the full value out of a machine it must be supervised or worked by a craftsman or artist who made it his servant ... If the manufacturers of England would call in the craftsmen and artists to their counsels all the world would gain.

Wilson's words were unfortunately not prophetic ones. With the end of the war, the pledge that soldiers would return to 'a land fit for heroes to live in' rapidly became a bitter jest during the depression of the 1920s and 1930s. In such a society there was no place for the incorporation of craftsmanship into the structure of industry. In this respect England was to be less fortunate than her foe. From the anarchic conditions of a defeated Germany was to spring the brief splendid flowering of the avant-garde design theories of the Bauhaus, which were to be of such importance to subsequent industrial developments until the suppression of the group by Hitler.

The nearest approach to Wilson's dream of cooperation between designer, craftsman and industry was, in fact, to evolve in Scandinavia, in societies relatively untouched both by the industrial revolution and the war. In Sweden these ideas had long been fostered by the Svenska Slöjdsföreningen (the Swedish Society for Industrial design) founded in the mid-nineteenth century, and active since the 1890s in developing a national style in the furniture, glass (the Orrefors factory), and the ceramics industry (the Rörstrand works). In Finland the craft revival had been slowly gathering impetus since the 1870s, and came into prominence with the work of Axel Gallen and Eliel Saarinen in the Paris Exhibition of 1900. Their work was to be consolidated in the active 'modern industrial art' policy of their shop, 'Iris', the springboard for the experimental work of men like Alvar Aalto in the 1930s. Denmark's distinguished silversmith Georg Jensen (1866–1935) began his work in 1905, creating a market for high quality, mass produced silver jewellery, while Kaare Klint (1884–1954) the architect, began in 1917 his anthropometric research in furniture design. The results, while using traditional forms and constructions from Chippendale and Shaker prototypes, were tailored to the needs of the human body. Klint's work

240 Collapsible deckchair in
teak and wicker designed by
Kaare Klint, 1933 (Victoria
and Albert Museum)

241 Chair by Alvar Aalto in
birch laminate, made for
Artek, *c*. 1929

240

241

242 Georg Jensen silver tea
pot, 1905 (Georg Jensen,
Copenhagen)

243 Vase in frosted glass,
c. 1930, painted by Nicke
Lindstrand for the Orrefors
glass company

242

243

influenced much later Scandinavian design. The same evolutionary process was followed in the career of Kay Bojesen, (1886–1958) who from the late 1910s gradually evolved rounded, functional forms for cutlery, and firmly repudiated any attempt to give a spurious air of hand craftsmanship to mass produced table wares.

Scandinavian factories between the wars were thus to come close to achieving the ideals of Sedding, Wright, Wilson and other more visionary Arts and Crafts theorists. In the words of Bojesen, 'The things we make should have life and heart in them, and be a joy to hold. They must be human, vital and warm'.

Developments in England, after the first world war, were very different. Empson's words:

> 'They drained an old dog dry
> But the exchange rills
> Of young dog's blood
> Bred but a month's desires'

can stand for the failure of industry to collaborate with designers, in spite of the efforts of the Design and Industries Association, founded in

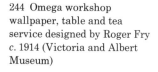

244 Omega workshop wallpaper, table and tea service designed by Roger Fry *c.* 1914 (Victoria and Albert Museum)

245 An early photograph
of Northfields Station prior
to its rebuilding in 1932
during Frank Pick's
administration of London
Transport

246 Northfields Station at the
time of its opening in 1933
(Victoria and Albert Museum)

247 London Transport
benches, designed during the
administration of Frank Pick,
or the triumph of design over
comfort. A seat for eight
people on a platform often
crowded with hundreds of
passengers

1914. The blood of the old dog of the Arts and Crafts movement, it was felt—*was* drained dry. The exchange rills of young dog's blood—the younger generation of designers—were at first rejected by industrial management which had become inured to the 'Holier than thou' attitude of the Arts and Crafts men schooled in a system antagonistic to industrial concerns.

There were, of course, exceptions to this depressing state of affairs. The Omega Workshops venture of Roger Fry (1800–1900) did much to clear the air of the old shibboleths, and the work of Frank Pick (1878–1942) in London Transport showed that design could be made to fulfil a vital role in a vast industrial concern. Gordon Russell, who did more than anyone to break down resistance to design in industry, achieved in the early radio cabinets for Murphy in 1931 the first notable success in overcoming this attitude, by creating a classic design for a new technological product. His autobiography *Designer's Trade*, is essential reading for those who wish to chart the slow beginnings of the acceptance of design in British industry, so aided by his work during the second world war in overseeing the production of Utility furniture, and setting up the Design Council.

'A new role for design in industry', the long looked-for promised land of the more far-sighted Arts and Crafts theorists proved a chimera. But, paradoxically, the movement could still produce a major craftsman and thinker of heroic stature. In a very real sense the greatest artist

248 Gordon Russell radio cabinet, 1932 (Victoria and Albert Museum)

249 Bernard Leach, bowl 1926
(Victoria and Albert Museum)

craftsman since William Morris, Bernard Leach, did not begin his work until the movement had virtually ended.

Bernard Leach, like William Morris, was one of those protean figures who is almost more important for what he represents, than for his actual productions. Born in 1887, much of his early life was spent in the far east. After his early studies of the making of stoneware in Japan he returned to this country in 1920 and with Shoji Hamada set up the famous pottery at St. Ives. This workshop was based on an attitude to the craftsman's role that echoed Morris's views, combined with a sensitivity to materials that came from the traditional Japanese potter's search for aesthetic purity of form. For some time he continued to produce stoneware in the Japanese manner, before turning his attention to the English slipware tradition. His two sons, David and Michael, and his many pupils still produce wares of remarkable quality. When he died in 1979 at the age of 92 Leach had become, like Morris, a legend in his own lifetime. He had done more to interest the public at large in pottery than any other man, by his work, teaching and books, in particular his guide to the practical and aesthetic experience of pottery *A Potter's Book*.

250

251

252

There have, of course, been many other important potter-teachers. William Staite Murray (1881–1962) held a contrasting view of pottery as an art form, without regard to any function, which has also been widely influential. Michael Cardew, Leach's first pupil, brought back from his years in Nigeria something of the dynamic power of the African pottery tradition.

Since the second world war the movement has greatly developed, and a generation of independent and experimental potters has arisen that has proved that there is room for the rarified intensity of a Lucie Rie, the power of Hans Coper, and the humour of a young contemporary potter like Andrew Wood.

250 Staithe Murray, vase

251 Lucie Rie, teapot, 1948

252 Michael Cardew, cider jar, 1936

253 Hans Coper, vase, 1938

(Illustrations: Victoria and Albert Museum)

254 Andrew Wood, Edward
Lear and Foss his cat 1979
(author's collection)

Like the theatre, the circus and the music hall, the Arts and Crafts
movement is always being pronounced dead by its older and disillusioned exponents. Listen for example to Arnold Wesker's character,
Dave, in the play *I'm Talking About Jerusalem*, first performed in 1960.
Dave Simmonds, an East End Jew, attempts to set up as an independent
furniture maker in a barn in Norfolk, but fails. In a speech of self-
justification he conveys the cynical attitude of his own age to the status
of the craftsman in society: 'You think I'm an artist craftsman? Nothing
of the sort. A designer? Not even that. Designers are ten a penny.... I've
reached the point where I can face the fact that I'm not a prophet... You
wanted us to grow to be giants, didn't you? The mighty artist-craftsman!
Face it—as an essential member of society I don't really count. I'm not
saying I'm useless, but machinery and modern techniques have come
about to make me the odd man out'.

255 David Pye, cherry-wood bowl, 1978 (author's collection)

Eight years later, in 1968, David Pye, Professor of Furniture Design at the Royal College of Art wrote in his book *The Nature and Art of Workmanship*, of the crafts,

... economics alone will never justify their continuation.

The crafts ought to provide the salt—and the pepper—to make the visible environment more palatable when nearly all of it will have been made by the workmanship of certainty. Let us have nothing to do with the idea that the crafts, regardless of what they make, are in some way superior to the workmanship of certainty, or a means of protest against it. That is a paranoia. The crafts ought to be a complement to industry.

Ten years later, we have come closer to this situation than seemed possible even a decade ago. The crafts have at last overcome their 'self importance of being earnest', and can be enjoyed in their own right, without being confusedly mixed up with Utopian worries about their role in an ideal society. The major figures of the Arts and Crafts movement can now be seen to have left a permanent legacy in their realization of the importance of crafts as a vital part of human life. This is reflected today in the students working up and down the country at craft centres with equipment and standards of teaching which were unthinkable a century ago. In 1940, just before he died, C. F. A. Voysey wrote, 'I have applied old traditions to new customs', and it is this principle which now predominates in craft teaching.

In 1970, the Annual General Meeting of the National Federation of Women's Institutes passed a resolution requesting that the Government treat the Crafts on a par with the Arts—for the explosive reason that 'they belong together like thunder and lightning!' Soon afterwards the many disparate groups of craftsmen up and down the country were linked in the Federation of British Craft Societies, meeting in the Art Worker's Guild's old home. So the history of the movement continues, with the practice of the arts and crafts more widespread today than ever. Like the desire for ornament and collecting, which can be observed working instinctively in a child selecting shells on a beach, man's urge to use hand and brain in the act of creating an individual artifact will always be with us. Although the Utopian marriage of the words 'Arts and Crafts' is now dissolved, we can still admire the ideals, if not all the work, of those to whom the phrase gave inspiration. These ideals can best be put into practice by buying or commissioning the work of the living craftsmen of our own day.

Bibliography

Isabelle Anscombe and Charlotte Gere *The Arts and Crafts in Britain and America.* Academy Editions, London, 1978

Charles Robert Ashbee *An Endeavour towards the Teaching of John Ruskin and William Morris.* Essex House Press, 1901

——*Craftsmanship in Competitive Industry.* Essex House Press, 1908

——*Modern English Silverwork.* Essex House Press, 1909. (Also available in a modern facsimile with essays by Alan Crawford and Shirley Bury, B. Weinreb, London, 1974

——*The Guild of Handicraft.* Essex House Press, 1909

——*Should We Stop Teaching Art?* B. T. Batsford, 1911

——*Where the Great City Stands.* Essex House Press and B. T. Batsford, London, 1917

——*Memoirs.* Unpublished typescript in the Victoria and Albert Museum Library

Henry Spencer Ashbee (*Pisanus Fraxi*) *Index of Forbidden Books* (n.d.). Sphere Paperbacks, London, 1969

——(anonymously) *Walter My Secret Life* (n.d.) edited by Stephen Marcus. London, 1969

Elizabeth Aslin *The Aesthetic Movement, Prelude to Art Nouveau.* Elek Books, London, 1969

M. H. Baillie Scott *A Small Country House*, 1897

——*Wohnhaus eines Kunstfreundes.* Meister der Innenkunst, Darmstadt, 1902

William Blake *The Complete Writings* edited by Geoffrey Keynes. Nonesuch Press, 1957, OUP, 1966

H. Allen Brooks *The Prairie School: Frank Lloyd Wright and his Midwest Contemporaries.* University of Toronto Press, Toronto and Buffalo, 1972

Anthea Callen *Angel in the Studio.* Astragal Books, London, 1979

G. K. Chesterton *The Napoleon of Notting Hill.* John Lane, London and New York, 1904

——*The Club of Queer Trades.* Harper and Bros, London and New York, 1905

William Cobbett *Rural Rides.* William Cobbett, London, 1830

T. J. Cobden-Sanderson *The Arts and Crafts Movement.* Hammersmith Publishing Society, Hammersmith, 1905

——*The Ideal Book.* Doves Press, Hammersmith, 1904

——*The Journals of Thomas James Cobden-Sanderson* (two volumes). R. Cobden-Sanderson, London, 1926

Gordon Craig *Gordon Craig's Book of Penny Toys.* Sign of the Rose, Hackbridge, 1899

——*The Portfolio*

Gillian Darley *Villages of Vision.* The Architectural Press, London, 1975

William De Morgan *Joseph Vance*

Charles Dickens *Hard Times.* Bradbury and Evan, London, 1854

Dr Christopher Dresser *The Art of Decorative Design.* London, 1862

——*Principles of Decorative Design.* London, 1873

William Empson *Collected Poems.* Chatto and Windus, London, 1955

Benjamin Ferrey *Recollections of Pugin*, 1861. New edition, edited by Clive Wainewright, Scolar Press, London, 1978

Ian Fletcher *Romantic Mythologies.* Routledge and Kegan Paul, London, 1964

William Gaunt and M. D. E. Clayton-Stamm *William De Morgan.* Studio Vista, London, 1971

W. S. Gilbert *Patience.* Chappell, London, 1881

T. A. Greeves *Bedford Park, the First Garden Suburb.* London, 1975

Thomas Hardy *Under the Greenwood Tree.* 1872

——Works in general

Malcolm Haslam *The Martin Brothers.* Richard Dennis, London, 1978

Sir Ambrose Heal *Workmanship* (n.d.)

Gerard Manley Hopkins *Poems* edited by Robert Bridges, 1918

——*A Selection of his Poems and Prose* edited by W. H. Gardiner. The Penguin Poets, 1956

Gertrude Jekyll *Home and Garden.* Longman, London, 1900

——*Wood and Garden.* Longman, London, 1899

Norman Jewson *By Chance I Did Rove.* Gordon Norwood at the Roundwood Press, Kineton, 1973

Edward Johnston *Writing and Illuminating and Lettering.* Pitman, London, 1906

Priscilla Johnston *Edward Johnston.* Faber and Faber, London, 1969

Owen Jones *Grammar of Ornament.* London, 1856

James D. Kornwolf *M. H. Baillie Scott and the Arts and Crafts Movement.* John Hopkins Press, Baltimore and London, 1972

Osbert Lancaster *Home Sweet Homes* John Murray, London, 1939, 1953

Bernard Leach *A Potter's Book*. Faber and Faber, London, 1940

W. R. Lethaby *Ernest Gimson His Life and Work*. Stratford-on-Avon, 1924

——*Philip Webb and his Works*. OUP, 1935

C. R. Mackintosh *Wohnhaus eines Kunstfreundes*. Meister der Innenkunst, Darmstadt, 1902

J. W. Mackail *The Life of William Morris*. London, 1899. Reissued in the World's Classics series, OUP, 1950

A. H. Mackmurdo *History of the Arts and Crafts Movement*. Unpublished typescript in the William Morris Gallery, Walthamstow

——*Autobiographic Notes*. Unpublished typescript in the William Morris Gallery, Walthamstow

——*The Human Hive: its life and law*. Watts and Co., London, 1926

——*A People's Charter*. Williams and Norgate, London, 1933

Stefan Tschudi Madson *Art Nouveau*. World University Library, Weidenfeld and Nicolson, London, 1967

William Morris *Collected Works* (24 volumes). Longman, Green and Co., London, 1910–1915

Hermann Muthesius *Das englische Haus*, 1905. Republished as *The English House* edited by Dennis Sharp, translated by Janet Seligman, Granada, London, 1979

Gillian Naylor *The Arts and Crafts Movement: a study of its sources, ideals and influence on design theory*. Studio Vista, London, 1971

Nikolaus Pevsner *Pioneers of the Modern Movement from William Morris to Walter Gropius*. Faber and Faber, London, 1936. Reissued as *Pioneers of Modern Design*, 1960

Gene Stratton Porter *The Harvester*. Hodder and Stoughton, London, Garden City, New York, 1911

Elinor Pugh *Arthur Hys Booke*. Illustrated manuscript in the William Morris Gallery, Walthamstow

A. W. N. Pugin *Contrasts*. London, 1936. Reissued by Leicester University Press, 1969

David Pye *The Nature and Art of Workmanship*. Cambridge University Press, 1968

John Ruskin *Complete Works* (29 volumes). Cook and Wedderburn, 1903

Gordon Russell *Designer's Trade*. Allen and Unwin, London, 1968

Isobel Spencer *Walter Crane*. Studio Vista, London, 1975

L. H. Sullivan *Ornament in Architecture*, 1892

Edward R. Taylor *Elementary Art Teaching*. Chapman and Hall, London, 1890

Henry Thoreau *Walden*

Robert Tressell *The Ragged Trousered Philanthropists*. Grant Richards, London, 1914

Arnold Wesker *Trilogy*. Penguin Books, Harmondsworth, 1972

Oscar Wilde *Letters* edited by R. Croft Cooke, 1962

Henry Wilson *Silverwork and Metalwork*, 1903

Frank Lloyd Wright *The Arts and Crafts of the Machine*

Exhibition Catalogues

'Arts and Crafts Exhibition Catalogues', 1888–1940

'The Arts and Crafts Movement, 1890–1930', Fine Art Society, London, 1973

'The Arts and Crafts Movement in America, 1876–1916' (Edited by R. J. Clark)

'Sidney Barnsley and the Cotswold School', Cheltenham Art gallery, 1977 (Mary Comino)

'Birmingham Gold and Silver 1773–1973', Birmingham City Museum and Art Gallery, 1973

'The Earthly Paradise—the work of the Birmingham Group', Fine Art Society, London, 1969

'Ernest Gimson', Leicester Museum and Art Gallery, 1969 (Lionel Lambourne)

'Liberty's 1875–1975', Victoria and Albert Museum, 1975

A scrapbook containing press cuttings relating to the 1916 Arts and Crafts Exhibition at the Royal Academy, London, Victoria and Albert Museum Library

'The Shakers', Victoria and Albert Museum, London, 1975

'Strict Delight, the work of Eric Gill', Manchester Art Gallery, 1980

'Victorian Church Art', Victoria and Albert Museum, London 1972

'Victorian and Edwardian Decorative Arts', Victoria and Albert Museum, London, 1952

'Victorian and Edwardian Decorative Arts', The Mandley-Read Collection, Royal Academy, London, 1972

'Vienna Secession: 1897–1970', London, 1971

Periodicals

'The Art Journal'

'The Art Workers' Quarterly'

'The Cabinet Maker'

'The Craftsman'

'The Furniture Gazette'

'The Hobby Horse'

'The Studio'

Index

256 Repoussé metalwork
executed at the Newlyn
Industrial Class. The artists of
the Newlyn School, grouped
around Stanhope A. Forbes,
had many links with the local
inhabitants of the picturesque
Cornish port. They founded
the Newlyn Industrial Class in
the 1880s as a means of
occupying the younger
fishermen in their spare time.
The Stanhope Forbes painting
shown on the back of the
book's jacket shows
metalwork such as this being
taught at the Class